Don't waste the crisis

Critical perspectives for a new economic model

Don't waste the crisis

Critical perspectives for a new economic model

Edited by Nicolas Pons-Vignon

International Labour Office • Geneva

Copyright © International Labour Organization 2010

First published 2010

Publications of the International Labour Office enjoy copyright under Protocol 2 of the Universal Copyright Convention. Nevertheless, short excerpts from them may be reproduced without authorization, on condition that the source is indicated. For rights of reproduction or translation, application should be made to ILO Publications (Rights and Permissions), International Labour Office, CH-1211 Geneva 22, Switzerland, or by email: pubdroit@ilo.org. The International Labour Office welcomes such applications.

Libraries, institutions and other users registered with reproduction rights organizations may make copies in accordance with the licences issued to them for this purpose. Visit www.ifrro.org to find the reproduction rights organization in your country.

Pons-Vignon, Nicolas (ed.)

Don't waste the crisis: Critical perspectives for a new economic model

Geneva, International Labour Office, 2010

economic recession / economic recovery / financial market / employment creation / trade union / trade union role / developed countries / developing countries

1 v.

03.04.3

ISBN: 978-92-2-123442-5

ILO Cataloguing in Publication Data

The designations employed in ILO publications, which are in conformity with United Nations practice, and the presentation of material therein do not imply the expression of any opinion whatsoever on the part of the International Labour Office concerning the legal status of any country, area or territory or of its authorities, or concerning the delimitation of its frontiers.

The responsibility for opinions expressed in signed articles, studies and other contributions rests solely with their authors, and publication does not constitute an endorsement by the International Labour Office of the opinions expressed in them.

Reference to names of firms and commercial products and processes does not imply their endorsement by the International Labour Office, and any failure to mention a particular firm, commercial product or process is not a sign of disapproval.

ILO publications and electronic products can be obtained through major booksellers or ILO local offices in many countries, or direct from ILO Publications, International Labour Office, CH-1211 Geneva 22, Switzerland. Catalogues or lists of new publications are available free of charge from the above address, or by email: pubvente@ilo.org

Visit our website: www.ilo.org/publns

Typeset by Magheross Graphics, France & Ireland *www.magheross.com*
Printed in Switzerland ATAR

Foreword

Dan Cunniah

The Great Recession is the worst global crisis since the Great Depression 80 years ago. The old globalization model failed. Business as usual is not an option. The damage has been done and the price for the excesses of the past will have to be paid. Whether this will be through a bitter deflationary process, the reduction of the welfare state, prolonged wage depression or a public investment and wage-led growth model based on a new balance between society, market and state is a policy choice. For trade unions, the choice is clear. The challenge for them is to mobilize in order to overcome powerful vested interests and to convince governments to make the right choice.

I am pleased to provide you with the first annual Global Labour Column yearbook, a collection of articles posted on a weekly basis on the Global Labour Column website. The Column aims to provide a forum in which labour movements and their allies around the world can connect, debate, and share knowledge and experiences. Through this sharing we hope to contribute to the development of fair and effective crisis response policies.

The Global Labour Column is the product of a close collaboration between ACTRAV and the Global Labour University (GLU) that brought together trade unionists and academics to devise new responses to the crisis. The Global Labour University is itself a collaboration of ACTRAV, trade unions, and a network of universities offering unique masters programmes to trade unionists around the world. GLU's courses are jointly developed by universities and workers' organizations and are aimed at students from trade union and social movement backgrounds in developed, developing and transition economies.

The production of the Global Labour Column and this subsequent yearbook arose from the identified need for labour-based, high-quality academic knowledge that could help workers' organizations respond to the current economic and financial crisis. Indeed, the growing complexity of a global economy requires academic knowledge and policy analysis that goes beyond workplace experience and classical industrial relations. To improve wages and working conditions crucially depends on issues outside the traditional areas of trade union activities. Rules and regulations for capital mobility, trade and taxation directly affect the world of work.

This is why the ILO's Global Jobs Pact has been proposing a new and comprehensive policy response to the crisis. Implementation of the Global Jobs Pact gives an additional urgency to the need to strengthen the knowledge base of trade unions both to respond to the crisis and to develop new paradigms and new ideas for sustainable globalization. I am very pleased that ACTRAV is able to contribute such a space for debate and knowledge-sharing, which will strengthen the knowledge and policy capacity of workers' organizations. I would like to thank in particular our partners at the Corporate Strategy and Industrial Development (CSID) research programme of the University of the Witwatersrand for coordinating and editing the weekly Global Labour Column and this book.

I hope you will find this collection of articles thought-provoking, and I encourage you to further engage in the debate by reading the articles on the Global Labour Column website.

Dan Cunniah is Director of the Bureau for Workers' Activities at the ILO. Prior to joining the ILO, Mr Cunniah was General Secretary of the Mauritius Labour Congress and from 1998 to 2004 he was Director of the Geneva office of the International Confederation of Free Trade Unions (ICFTU) and Secretary of the Workers' group at the ILO.

Contents

Foreword v
Preface ix
Acknowledgements xiii
Introduction: Beyond neoliberalism? xv

PART I   Public investment and wages: Leading recovery 1
   Frank Hoffer / Don't waste the crisis: The case for sustained public
      investment and wage-led recovery policies 3
   John Evans / Creating jobs now and changing the economic growth
      model for the future 9
   Andrew Jackson / Beyond "stimulus": Fiscal policy after the Great Recession . 13
   Engelbert Stockhammer / Profits, banks and the state: How to get
      investment going again 17
   Patrick Belser / Why we should care about wages 21
   Heiner Flassbeck / Putting employment security first will diminish demand:
      A warning from Germany 25

PART II   The need to reform global finance 29
   Christoph Scherrer / Finance capital will not fade away on its own 31
   Pierre Habbard / Taxing financial transactions: The right thing to do when
      you owe $600 billion a year and have lost control over global finance .. 37
   Raymond Torres / Global Financial Crisis 2.0 43
   Ekkehard Ernst / The end of an era: What comes after financialization and
      what will be the consequences for labour? 49

PART III   The economic crisis and challenges to national policies 53
   Neva Seidman Makgetla / The international economic crisis and
      development strategy: A view from South Africa 55
   Alessandra Mezzadri / The global footloose proletariat and the financial
      crisis: Reflections on the contradictions of export-oriented
      industrialization in India 61

Ronald Janssen / Greece-bashing is hiding the obvious: Monetary union urgently needs economic union 65
Robert Kyloh / Riding your luck and adopting the right policies: Why the Australian economy has rebounded strongly 69

PART IV Can the economic crisis lead to a redefinition of labour strategies? . 73
Gregory Albo / Unions and the crisis: Ways ahead? 75
Cédric Durand / New challenges for labour as growth prospects fade away . 81
Andrew Watt / Making its voice heard: A role for the labour movement in policies for recovery 85
Renana Jhabvala / Financial crises, the informal economy and workers' unions 89
Martin Upchurch / The crisis of social democratic trade unionism in Western Europe 93

Preface

Sharan Burrow

The weekly Global Labour Columns published here are critical essays that provide new perspectives on the global crisis. The authors, from trade unions and academia, discuss what needs to change in society and how labour has to adapt to overcome the legacy of a failed globalization regime.

The world is still in the midst of an economic crisis of unprecedented scale, and talk about a recovery is premature. Indeed, the number of unemployed is still rising, and neither private consumption nor private investment is strong enough to pull the economy out of stagnation. Economists agree that withdrawing fiscal stimuli now would most likely push the world economy into a double-dip recession. However, the speculative dynamics of inadequately regulated global financial markets and domestic budgetary pressures increasingly limit the fiscal space for many governments to continue expansionary policy.

The international community largely succeeded in avoiding a financial meltdown but failed to implement any lessons learned from this crisis. The economic paradigm of the last 30 years resulted in a decline of workers' income, huge global trade and financial imbalances, growing inequalities, unsustainable consumer debt, declining real investment and an oversized financial sector divorced from the real economy. Thanks to cheap government money, stock markets have recovered from huge losses, but housing markets are still depressed. As the former largely constitutes the wealth of the rich and the latter the investment of ordinary men and women, inequality continues to grow even during this crisis in many countries.

Frequent destructive financial bubbles are the basis of the current economic regime. The unprecedented growth of "financial weapons of mass destruction" (Warren Buffet) led to the build-up of gigantic cathedrals of virtual money that were beyond imagination. Pumping money into the system without making fundamental economic changes carries not only the risk but the likelihood that the volatility in the global economy will increase further and create another huge bubble.

The deficit-financed bail-outs have so far postponed the question of who shall pay for the crisis. Governments are under pressure to contain and reduce debt levels in the medium term. Public investment, public sector employment and welfare state provisions are increasingly becoming the target of budget consolidation. Savings in public health expenditure and in pensions will now pay for the excesses of the financial markets. Such a strategy is unfair and threatens to destroy the social cohesion of societies. Furthermore, pro-cyclical fiscal tightening and further decline in purchasing power due to lower transfer incomes may lead to long-term stagnation. Deficit and debt as a share of GDP stand to grow further, as pro-cyclical budget-cuts would be overcompensated by a decline in tax revenues and lack of growth in a depressed economy.

In the current situation, either competitive or cooperative responses to the crisis are conceivable. The competitive response would mean that countries and companies try to maintain and extend their export market share through an aggressive price war. The consequences of such a response would be brutal wage cuts, export subsidies, export-orientated tax reform such as shifting tax revenues to VAT and the depreciation of currencies. While export surplus makes perfect sense for individual countries, clearly not all countries can have a surplus. Indeed, it is a zero-sum game: one country's surplus must be another country's deficit. In reality, however, not countries but companies are competing. The issue is not to artificially increase the costs of highly productive enterprises, but to raise the overall level in order to ensure a growth in imports, a growth of aggregate demand and a rebalancing of the global economy. In surplus countries, companies should not sell less, but citizens and/or governments should buy more.

Despite all the lip service to free trade and non-protectionist policies, the competitive option is the fastest route to a breakdown of the open global economic system. Those countries that are unwilling or unable to lower their people's living standards as rapidly as others will have no option but to take protective anti-dumping measures against those who want to export themselves out of the crisis.

A cooperative solution would instead entail concerted action to strengthen aggregate final demand, reverse the wage slide, extend social security and rebalance economies globally. Regulating and reducing the speculative nature of the financial industry and resurrecting the capacity to tax capital and wealth are critical elements of this approach. It would also put decent work and social justice at the centre of a recovery strategy. As such, there is a political choice to be made between a sustainable, income-led recovery strategy and a competitive race to the bottom.

Those who benefited from neoliberal globalization and financialization of our economies show no inclination to take any responsibility for the current state of the global economy. Indeed, they lobby vigorously against any attempts to protect societies against casino capitalism, and they benefit greatly from the support of an army of think tanks and so-called independent academic researchers. However, many of these research publications are in fact thinly disguised advocacy for self-interest. The systemic underfunding of public universities means that knowledge production itself has become increasingly privatized and interest-led. These experts continue to prescribe the same old medicine that killed the patient and made the doctors rich: flexible labour markets, lower taxes, less government spending, free capital markets and a lofty regulatory hand on financial markets are still on the agenda as if nothing happened. A recovery on these terms, promoted by the financial sector and the corporate world, will result in working people paying for this crisis through higher unemployment, lower wages or declining wages share, social expenditure cuts, fewer public services and increased consumption taxes.

Trade unions thus face a tremendous challenge. The pressure on wages and employment requires immediate responses and solutions. Often unions have no choice but to negotiate the sharing of pain during crisis. Simultaneously, however, they have to be a driving force in shaping a future with a fairer national and global economy. We cannot do the first and not the second, or vice versa. Just focusing on defensive measures means steady further retreat. Without policy changes, working conditions will deteriorate and trade unions will face increasing difficulties with organizing workers, strengthening bargaining power and advancing progressive policies. Just focusing on the big picture of fundamental change and not engaging in the daily business of sometimes bitter concessionary compromises is no answer either. Today's problems need to be dealt with today.

Realists say that "people want solutions and not visions", but there are no lasting solutions without inspiring new visions. In this respect the crisis is also an opportunity for rethinking economic and social policies. The old regime failed and it is now the time to think beyond business as usual. To respond to the current global economic crisis, we need economic policies that give priority to full employment, fair income distribution, high-quality public services, income security and long-term investment to transform our economies to environmental and social sustainability. This will not be possible without progressive taxation, a financial transactions tax, tightly regulated financial markets, a developmental trade regime, green industrial policies, extended collective bargaining coverage, universal application of protective labour legislation and comprehensive social security provisions.

Such a change requires new ideas, inspired visions and political will. The Global Labour Column is an invitation to participate in this open deliberation process as it provides a forum for developing and debating new ideas and visions that respond proactively to the crisis. Envisaging a more sustainable future starts with a critical understanding of the causes of the crisis. Putting new ideas on the firing line of public debate is a further step to overcoming the failed wisdom of economic and political orthodoxy. The authors of this compendium offer innovative ideas on wage-led recovery strategies, forward-looking public investment and industrial solutions, new concepts for development and coordinated international policies. This publication is a timely and inspiring contribution to an urgently needed agenda for change.

Sharan Burrow is President of the International Trade Union Congress (ITUC) and serves on the Governing Body of the International Labour Organization (ILO) as the Workers' spokesperson on the Employment and Social Policy Committee. She has been President of the Australian Council of Trade Unions since 2000. She led the Workers' group in the negotiations of the Global Jobs Pact at the International Labour Conference in 2009. For many years she has been a strong voice for fairer globalization and better regulation of the global markets in a wide range of national and international forums.

Acknowledgements

The present volume and the Global Labour Column were launched by the Global Labour University to strengthen the debate about labour responses to the global crisis. This initiative would not have been possible without, first of all, the many authors who wrote excellent articles. It is also indebted to the tireless work of Samantha Ashman, Seeraj Mohamed, Phumzile Ncube, Susan Newman and Nicolas Pons-Vignon, the editorial team at the Corporate Strategy and Industrial Development (CSID) research programme at the University of the Witwatersrand. Harald Kroeck as webmaster of the Global Labour Column and the support of ACTRAV, particularly the contributions of Claire Hobden and Frank Hoffer, were also vital to its success.

We would also like to acknowledge others who worked on *Don't waste the crisis*: Werner Arnold, who designed the cover; Beatrice Reynolds of Magheross Graphics, who did the page design and typesetting; and Chris Edgar and Charlotte Beauchamp, who handled the book's production.

Finally, we would like to thank the Federal Ministry for Economic Cooperation and Development of Germany for its financial support, and Sharan Burrow and other trade unionists for their political support and encouragement, both in terms of this book and the weekly Global Labour Column.

Introduction: Beyond neoliberalism?

Nicolas Pons-Vignon

For the generation that came of age in the 1990s, the belief in the labour movement's ability to inspire progressive change collapsed soon after the Berlin Wall. Not unlike the Wall, this belief had been seriously shaken during the 1970s and 1980s, which saw the rise of neoliberalism from Chile to the United Kingdom and, thanks to the Washington-based international financial institutions, to much of the developing world. Jan Breman (1995), in a biting analysis of the triumphant World Bank's *World Development Report* on "Workers in an integrating world", notes that the Bank saw "drastic restructuring in the balance of power in favour of capital" as a necessary condition for both economic growth and poverty reduction. Written at the height of the Washington Consensus, the report represented an arrogant dismissal of workers as political actors. Only if they would keep quiet, letting the invisible hand of the market decide how many shillings (3, maybe) to put in their pockets, would their lives improve. While some economists and politicians were genuinely convinced that neoclassical economic theory could offer an alternative to the previously dominant Keynesian paradigm, it has since appeared that, behind the market fundamentalism justified "scientifically" by economists (such as those of the Public Choice School) eager to show that governments and unions were predatory self-interested agents, lay the formidable enterprise of shifting the balance of forces in society towards private business and particularly capital holders. As Harvey (2006) points out, far from being a *technical* choice over allocative efficiency, neoliberalism is first and foremost a *political* enterprise aimed at restoring the power of capital. It does so in two ways: first by shifting economic resources back to owners of capital, and second by weakening the capacity of organized labour to resist policy changes in the workplace or in public policy.

At odds with the professed neutrality of neoclassical economics, neoliberal policies have actively promoted the interests of large (often Western, in developing countries) companies by extending the realm where they could invest (through privatization and liberalization) and the conditions under which they were able to do so (repatriation of profits, low taxation and regulation).[1] Such measures have been accompanied by the systematic undermining of labour's capacity to constitute itself as a political force that could challenge these policies, as exemplified by the aggressive behaviour of Margaret Thatcher's Government towards the miners' strikes of the 1980s in the United Kingdom. The victory of the Conservatives in this country paved the way for far-reaching deregulation of the labour market, which resulted in widespread precariousness for working people. This not only made life harder but also undermined the strength of unions, since the number of workers employed in permanent contracts started dropping rapidly. In light of these facts, it remains a puzzling reality that in most developed countries critical views did not catch the imagination of people and that majorities repeatedly voted for minority interests. The result of these policies has thus been a massive skewing of income towards the very rich, with remarkably little resistance in the process. The extent of this growing inequality in the United States can be strikingly observed in the long-term evolution of the income share of the top 1 per cent (see figure).[2]

For many years, neoliberal policies have undermined the living conditions of workers, from Chile to the United States and Africa, and with a possibly

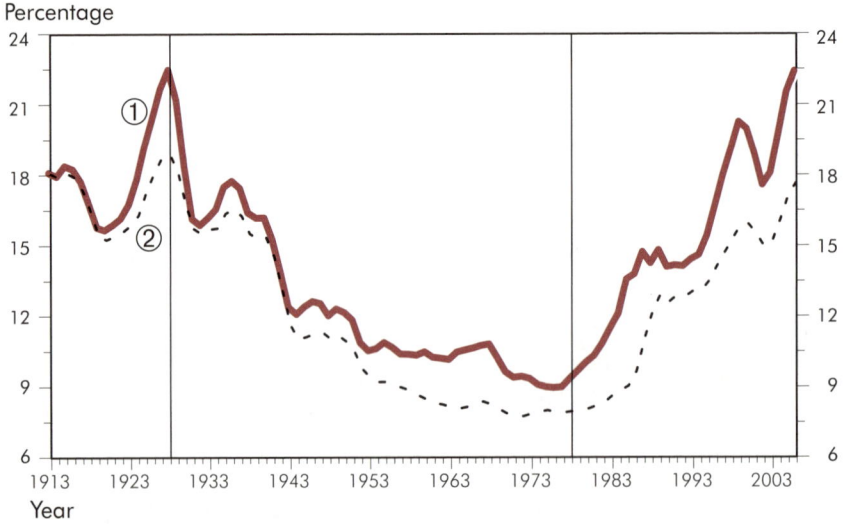

United States: Income share of the top 1 per cent, 1913–2006

Notes: [1] = including realized capital gains; and [2] = excluding capital gains. Three-year moving averages.
Source: Palma, 2009.

greater impact than anywhere else in former communist countries. The current crisis confirms what many heterodox economists have been arguing for many years, namely that neoliberal policies are not only bad for workers, but also for growth and development. Amsden (2010) thus points out the paradox of their continued dominance in the face of a proven inability to generate higher growth than the policies they replaced. As is apparent in the table below, per capita growth performances have been superior in the period 1950–80 than in the period 1980–2000 everywhere *but* in South Asia and in the United States. In the latter, as has been discussed above, growing inequality has meant that growth has disproportionately benefited the richest, with the "bottom 90 per cent" of earners in the United States having actually experienced stagnation between 1971 and 2005 (Palma, 2009). Moreover, China and India, two

GDP growth rate and GDP per capita growth rate, 1950–2000

Region	GDP growth rates		GDP per capita growth rates	
	1950–80 %	1980–2000 %	1950–80 %	1980–2000 %
Western Europe	4.20	2.20	3.24	2.06
United States	3.47	3.45	1.79	1.93
Japan	7.10	2.65	5.50	2.12
Developed countries average	**4.12**	**2.46**	**3.06**	**1.97**
Eastern Europe and USSR	5.46	0.41	4.31	−0.85
Latin America	4.75	2.32	2.15	0.55
Asia				
East Asia	6.90	5.83	4.11	3.43
South Asia	3.98	5.05	1.21	2.49
Middle East	8.04	2.03	3.01	0.47
Africa				
North Africa	5.32	3.56	2.30	1.25
Africa, South of Sahara	3.70	2.61	1.20	−0.12
Developing countries average	**5.06**	**3.02**	**2.04**	**0.75**

Sources: World Tables, Johns Hopkins University, 1980, 1994.
World Development Indicators, World Bank, 2002.
World Bank online data (http://www.worldbank.org).

countries which seem to be steadily emerging despite the crisis, have adopted development policies markedly different from those recommended by the Washington Consensus, even if their labour policies have been more aligned with it. And the current economic crisis offers convincing evidence that the growth path of the leading neoliberal countries was premised on very shaky foundations.

Depleted growth, stagnating income for workers and their families in many countries, and at the same time a massive enrichment of the wealthiest, in particular capital owners in the West: the outcome of neoliberal policies is such that its continued dominance can indeed be astonishing. The collapse of the Soviet bloc and the deep disillusion with state-managed planned economies has certainly played an important part in the difficulties experienced by the labour movement to resist and propose an alternative to neoliberal globalization. This was particularly clear in the case of South Africa, where the fall of the apartheid regime, achieved largely through worker mobilization, took place in an environment where the international and internal pressures to follow the neoliberal trend proved too strong to resist for the new leadership.

Despite several crises related to burst "bubbles" of over-valued assets, it is only with the current crisis that a consensus – claiming unlikely allies such as Alan Greenspan – is emerging to argue that the entire finance-driven system of accumulation is in need of regulatory reform. However, while growing numbers recognize its deep flaws, many still favour superficial changes in line with Guiseppe Tomasi di Lampedusa's ultimate advice for the continuity of power in a time of crisis: "everything must change so that everything can stay the same". While finance has been a locus of incredible accumulation over the last 25 years, it must be emphasized that this cannot be reduced to harmless speculation. At the core of finance, of its inflated assets and their over-inflated derivatives, lies the way in which neoliberal capitalism has been able to supplement the loss of demand linked to the depleted incomes of working people by trapping them in ownership of expensive yet worthless homes (or other goods) through credit. Indeed, it is thanks to credit that demand levels have been maintained for so many years; the fact that this credit growth was entirely linked to self-fulfilling fantasies regarding asset values signals an irrationality which ridicules the claims to science often heard in mainstream economics departments. Moreover, the hardships many average informal and formal workers and their families are suffering in the crisis has shed a particularly crude light on the readiness of states to invest hitherto unavailable billions of dollars in bailouts, which have often not even been used to re-assert control over the banking system.

This book and the Global Labour Column hope to make an important and engaged contribution to the public debate on some of the issues discussed above, but also to stimulate an exchange of ideas contributing to the rebuilding of the union movement. Moving towards more inclusive and more equal societies requires stronger unions and a broad-based movement for change. The column offers a unique meeting point to progressive academics, from universities, trade unions and international organizations, and activists and trade union leaders. The title of the book – *Don't waste the crisis* – is meant to emphasize that, if one good thing can come out of this crisis, it is to reopen debate on the direction of economic policy and on how people are employed. Now that the claim that worker-adverse policies were "good for growth" has been dismissed, it is essential to join forces for a new economic dispensation, which will ensure economic development with decent job opportunities. It is time to question the central policies of neoliberalism and their assumptions, such as the "requirement" for the state and social security systems to spend less. Union members are among the first victims of state spending cuts. Challenging such policies requires economic strategies and political mobilization that are focused on quality jobs, fair wages, comprehensive public services, political as well as industrial democracy and long-term social and environmental sustainability, rather than on the narrow interests of a financially affluent minority. But it is also time to discuss, honestly and in a constructive manner, the shortcomings of trade unions when they have sometimes failed to defend the weakest workers; and to propose ways in which unions can be inclusive and at the forefront of social and economic progress.

The articles reproduced in this book touch on a variety of issues, and come from different perspectives. Some have been written by academics (such as Gregory Albo or Alessandra Mezzadri), others by trade union economists (such as Andrew Jackson) or leaders (such as John Evans or Renana Jhabvala). Actually, the essential thrust of the Global Labour Column is to offer a critical space where contradictory opinions can be expressed and can hopefully enrich each other. It is our hope that the crisis will give a new impetus to attempts to connect workers, unions and intellectuals from all over the world. If this book can inspire its readers to follow the Column and participate in it, it will have made a valuable contribution.

The Column has a rich diversity of contributors, who adopt very different perspectives, and sometimes present contradicting analyses and recommendations. This collection is structured in four parts. In the first, several contributions advocate a public investment and wage-led recovery, emphasizing that the crisis has happened in the wake of years of lower taxation for the rich.

In the second, the authors assert that no national strategy will be sustainable if global finance is not profoundly reformed, by limiting speculation while reorienting investment towards productive activities. Different national responses to the crisis are discussed in the third part, stressing the importance of a solid national grounding of any discussion on economic policy – even when this involves the need for a regional approach, as in the case of Greece. Finally, in the last part, a number of contributions seek to answer the crucial yet complex question of how to redefine labour strategies in the face of the crisis. While some emphasize the need to adapt to changing macroeconomic conditions, all concur that labour needs to have a more confident and more inclusive approach, not least towards informal and unprotected workers.

Notes

[1] Harvey (ibid.) shows how the very first series of measures adopted by Paul Bremer in Iraq in 2003 all revolved around the opening of the Iraqi economy to US corporate investment, while "[t]he right to unionize and strike … were strictly circumscribed" (p. 10). One can appreciate the sense of priorities that inhabited the US Government in the immediate aftermath of a war waged in the name of freedom, when much of the country's critical infrastructure had been destroyed by bombs.

[2] Gabriel Palma, the source of this graph, argues that neoliberalism is the art of achieving such "redistribution" in a democracy.

References

Amsden, A. 2010. "Say's Law, poverty persistence, and employment neglect", in *Journal of Human Development and Capabilities*, Vol. 11, No. 1, pp. 57–66.

Breman, J. 1995. "Labour, get lost: A late-capitalist manifesto", in *Economic and Political Weekly*, 16 Sep., pp. 2294–2300.

Harvey, D. 2006. "Neo-liberalism and the restoration of class power", in *Spaces of global capitalism* (London, Verso).

Palma, J.G. 2009. "The revenge of the market on the rentiers: Why neo-liberal reports of the end of history turned out to be premature", in *Cambridge Journal of Economics*, Vol. 33, No. 4, pp. 829–869.

Nicolas Pons-Vignon is Senior Research Fellow with the Corporate Strategy and Industrial Development (CSID) research programme, University of the Witwatersrand, South Africa. His research focuses on industrial development and policy in South Africa, as well as on labour and poverty. He is the founder and course director of the annual African Programme for Rethinking Development Economics (APORDE; http://www.aporde.org.za). Prior to joining CSID, Nicolas was a consultant at the OECD Development Centre and worked for an international non-governmental organization (NGO) in London, Morocco and Paris. Nicolas is completing a Ph.D. on labour casualization in the forestry sector in South Africa at the École des Hautes Études en Sciences Sociales in Paris.

PART I

Public investment and wages: Leading recovery

Don't waste the crisis: The case for sustained public investment and wage-led recovery policies

Frank Hoffer

Returning to the pre-crisis world after timely, targeted and temporary government interventions as advocated by the Organisation for Economic Co-operation and Development (OECD) and others is risky and a waste of public funds. Structural changes in income distribution, taxation and capital markets are needed to address the fundamental causes of the crisis and put social justice and decent work at the centre of a crisis response.

Root causes of the global economic crisis

In recent decades, wages and transfer incomes have not grown in line with productivity in most countries. In fact, institutional and legal capital and labour market changes, combined with aggressive, short-term profit-maximization strategies, enabled the owners of private enterprises and financial capital to appropriate most of society's productivity gains. Moreover, threats of relocation or disinvestment resulted in labour market deregulation and casualization of employment. Such global capital mobility led to the rise of tax havens, transfer pricing and tax competition, reducing the ability of governments to tax capital, thus driving down tax rates and regulation levels. Meanwhile, the high profit rate in the financial industry put pressure on the real economy to produce similar results for shareholders. Thus, the profits of the financial bubble economy became the benchmark for the real economy.

In sum, while income differentials have widened, the tax burden has shifted to employees and consumers, further reducing purchasing power of the people. Throughout the world indecent, precarious and informal employment is increasing.

In many countries, open capital markets overly constrain government's ability to pursue expansionary fiscal policy, as any increase in inflation would trigger capital outflows and ultimately risk a currency crisis. These capital market constraints, combined with the declining ability to tax, reduced government's space for public expenditure, while low wages limited private consumer demand. Nevertheless, overall demand stayed high as rapidly growing private deficit spending backed by asset bubbles disguised the long-term unsustainability of growing imbalances in distribution and trade. It created the illusion that consumption can rise despite a declining wage share, and that wage increases below productivity growth are "only" a problem of social justice, not an economic policy issue.

As long as asset prices go up, a bubble seems to be a free lunch where everybody gains. However, the bubble, like any pyramid scheme, can only continue if more and more people join. The bubble itself creates a need to loosen credit criteria further: as the ratio between actual income and asset prices grows, credit conditions need to be softened to draw new entrees in the (real estate) market. Financial irresponsibility has to grow.

> *As long as asset prices go up, a bubble seems to be a free lunch where everybody gains*

When the bubble burst, it did not just hit the bubble economies; countries with an export surplus-led strategy, priding themselves on their solid financial policies, also saw their "beggar thy neighbour" policies collapsing. They could no longer offset their lack of internal demand through ever-growing export surpluses. The export machines came to a standstill. The export champions realized that they had exchanged real goods against fancy but toxic pieces of paper. Instead of sharing productivity gains fairly in society, they were wasted.

Saving the financial system by bailing out the irresponsible banks is insufficient to address the underlying imbalances and to increase aggregate demand. During the economic downturn, private investment will remain sluggish. Over-indebted consumers cannot continue to spend beyond their means. There is no alternative to continued substantial countercyclical monetary and fiscal state intervention.

But state intervention can only be lastingly successful if accompanied by policy measures to correct the dysfunctional wage developments of the past decades, to build a genuinely fair and progressive tax base and change the dysfunctional global capital markets.

A decent work response

In a global economy, coordinated global responses are the optimal solution. This requires national and international rules for capital and labour markets. The ILO's Global Jobs Pact offers a policy framework to meet these needs.

Investing in the future, creating employment and increasing the social wage

Under the conditions of a slump, public investment has a higher employment intensity than tax cuts. The provision of universal quality public services and infrastructure is key to reducing inequality, building inclusive societies and increasing opportunities for the poor. Universal quality education, health service, affordable housing, and other freely accessible public services reduce the need for individual savings and increase the proportion of people's disposable income.

> *Freely accessible public services reduce the need for individual savings and increase the proportion of people's disposable income*

Preventing wage deflation and promoting wage-led recovery

Increased public investment must be complemented by institutional measures to avoid wage deflation, reduce wage inequality, ensure that productivity gains translate to higher wages, and thus to ensure a sustainable consumption pattern. Combining centralized or coordinated collective bargaining with minimum wage legislation is most suitable to establish a wage floor and compress wage differentials. Increasing the wage share and strengthening the wages of low-income workers in particular leads to an increase of overall consumption, as poor households spend a higher share of their income. Simultaneously, precarious employment relationships must be limited as they have been used to circumvent labour rights and collective bargaining agreements. Labour clauses in public contracts must request contractors and subcontractors to pay the prevailing collective bargaining wage rate. Moreover, public sector employment must be increased and public sector wage levels must be maintained to serve as an additional wage anchor.

The state has to combat employer's aggression against the desire of workers to form or join a trade union. It needs to level the playing field through legal mechanisms of extending collective bargaining coverage and worker representation at the workplace. Any bailout or state subsidies must hinge on worker participation in the restructuring through collective bargaining processes and agreements.

Maintaining and extending social protection

Social security systems are the fastest and most efficient way to provide income replacement for workers in a crisis situation. Comprehensive social security systems act as automatic stabilizers and must be extended during an economic downturn to stabilize income levels and overall consumer demand.

In developing countries without comprehensive social security systems, a social floor that includes a basic pension, child benefits, access to health care and temporary employment guarantee schemes or cash transfers for the under- and unemployed is urgently needed to lift millions of people out of poverty. It contributes to increasing demand and is a necessary complement to any effective minimum wage legislation.

Finally, governments must protect retirement savings. Pay as you go systems are clearly less vulnerable through capital market volatility. Any pension scheme – private or public – must be legally obliged to guarantee at least a minimum rate of return equivalent to government bonds.

Making the necessary global structural changes

The suggested measures will be difficult to implement and impossible to sustain without restructuring the global financial system that has propelled the failed economic regime.

Regaining the ability to tax capital

Tax havens must be closed. To solve this issue, banks that work in tax havens, either directly or through subsidiaries, or that engage in other tax theft operations, should be barred from major US or European Union (EU) financial centres. Multinationals should be required to report their global profits and pay a unitary tax, treating as a unit all the business that is done under one ownership, then estimating what proportion of their income was earned in a specific country and applying its national tax to that income. Transfer pricing and financial dislocation would become rather unattractive. Wealth and heritage taxes and marginal tax rates on high income must be increased to rebalance the tax burden in society and increase the purchasing power of ordinary citizens. Property taxes on high value real estate would be a first step that could be introduced relatively easily even at the national level.

Downsizing speculative and high risk activities of the financial industry

A small tax on stock market transactions would abolish unproductive financial market speculation based on minimal margins and high leverage. A high capital gains tax on short-term profits would reduce incentives for speculative trade in financial markets. Higher reserve requirements for banks and more conservative rules for mortgages reduce the probability of asset bubbles. Banks can only be allowed to operate as private enterprises if they bear the risks of their investment and never become too big to fail. A diverse banking system – incorporating state-guaranteed savings banks, clearly mandated public development banks and private banks – is needed to reduce the institutional lobby and blackmail power of the financial industry. Rating agencies that are fully independent from the financial industry have to ensure better risk assessment. Investor protection against toxic products must be provided through compulsory state certification of all financial products. Risk-taking by pension funds needs to be limited by insisting on a guaranteed minimum rate of return.

Conclusions

Without structural changes as proposed above, we risk wasting today's crisis. The unconditional promise of governments for universal bailouts after the collapse of Lehman Brothers has indeed increased the moral hazard problem. Pumping money into the system without addressing the causes of global imbalances is dangerous and unsustainable, and may soon lead us into another financial crisis. However, governments will have much less financial firepower, then, because the ammunition was used for another Wall Street firework display instead of closing the casino.

Frank Hoffer is Senior Research Officer at the Bureau for Workers' Activities (ACTRAV) of the ILO. He is international coordinator of the Global Labour University and represents the ILO on the Steering Committee of the International Center for Development and Decent Work.

Creating jobs now and changing the economic growth model for the future

John Evans

The financial crisis, which took a dramatic turn for the worse in September 2008, has plunged the world into a deep recession in which workers in industrialized and emerging countries are losing their jobs, their homes and their pensions. For those in developing countries, the consequences are even more acute. According to the ILO, globally, 60 million more workers will become unemployed this year, with an extra 240 million workers earning below €1 a day.

The collapse of production in the last quarter of 2008 and the first half of 2009 was on a scale unseen since the 1930s. The talk of the "green shoots" of recovery is more a dream of financial markets than reality for the workers losing their jobs. There is a vicious circle where unemployment – which almost doubled in OECD countries in 2009 and will continue to rise to above 9 per cent in 2010 – also leads to collapsing house prices, driving asset prices down, pushing the financial sector into further crisis and leading to further bankruptcies and job losses in the real economy. We have not yet reached the bottom as far as unemployment is concerned, and the OECD World of Work report published in December 2009 warns, on the basis of current policies, that industrialized country unemployment will not return to pre-crisis levels before 2013.

"Green shoots" of recovery are more a dream of financial markets than reality for the workers losing their jobs

Unless governments take the unemployment crisis more seriously, the 2010s will become a "lost decade". The global trade union movement is united in its determination to ensure that this does not happen.

In the short term, we have sought to protect our members, workers at large and their families from the worst effects of the crisis. In this, we have pushed for governments to take the lead and insisted that there can be no "exit" from stimulus measures until there is recovery in the labour market. The Global Unions' statements to the G20 Summits have set out the criteria that should be applied to stimulus, recovery plans and public investment, in particular:

- action must be fast;
- action must make a maximum impact in creating jobs;
- action must be socially just and protect the worst off; and
- action must be transformational in terms of helping to resolve climate change, raise productivity and skills for the future and get economies back onto a higher growth path.

The International Monetary Fund (IMF), the OECD and the G20 Pittsburgh Summit came out against prematurely withdrawing economic stimulus – this much we welcomed. The US administration has just agreed to release TARP funds (Troubled Asset Relief Program) to create jobs and the Hatayama Administration in Japan has announced a recovery package. But much more is needed. Action has to be targeted at having the maximum impact on employment, rather than wasting money on tax cuts for the wealthy or on corporate tax cuts.

The Trade Union Advisory Committee (TUAC) to the OECD and the International and European Trade Union Confederations (ITUC and ETUC) have called for a real recovery plan that commits a further 1 per cent of GDP in public investment in each of the next three years and is coordinated internationally. Our estimates indicate that this would slow and then stabilize the otherwise catastrophic rise in unemployment.

Far more of the stimulus programmes have to be devoted to keeping workers in economic activity until investment measures have their impact. On average, only 3–5 per cent of the expenditure in stimulus plans has been devoted to active labour market measures – at the most the figure is 8 per cent. We need schemes such as intelligent work sharing where workers are kept employed until demand picks up, if necessary, with short-time working compensated by state support for training and retraining. Measures also have to be targeted at young people, to avoid having a cohort, if not a generation, of our youth leaving education, moving into unemployment and being passed over by employers when the recovery comes. The ILO Global Jobs Pact, which was agreed on a tripartite basis at the ILO last June and endorsed at Pittsburgh, must now lead to action by governments.

At the Pittsburgh Summit it was announced that a G20 labour ministers meeting would be held in Washington in April 2010 with the involvement of the ILO, business and labour. But there is a need to act before then. Trade unions are demanding that a permanent tripartite G20 Working Group be established to act on and monitor unemployment.

We should all be concerned at what model of growth emerges from the crisis. Governments are already talking of the need for an "exit strategy" from the crisis that puts into reverse what they describe as the "exceptional" policies of the past year. The question that must be debated is "exit to what?". The crisis was not just another financial crisis that can be avoided in the future by tighter financial regulation alone. The "Shadow G*N*" group chaired by Joseph Stiglitz and Jean-Paul Fitoussi has noted that this crisis is unprecedented for at least four reasons:

- *First*, it is truly global in nature – global markets have spread the crisis most to those dependent on exports.
- *Second*, the crisis is profoundly unfair – those suffering most from its effects were least responsible for its creation. It comes on top of a general increase in inequality, a shift from wages to profits over the past 15 years across the globe and a transfer of market risk from employers and governments on to workers and their families as seen in the wave of privatization of pensions, health care, and public services.
- *Third*, the causes of the crisis were structural – the imbalances in the model of global growth and inequality in incomes – as well as the consequences of insufficient financial regulation, if we can speak of "regulation" at all.
- And *fourth*, the crisis was produced by an ideology of market fundamentalism – a belief in the self-regulating properties of markets and denigration of the role of the state and public welfare systems.

It is imperative that the new policies are put in place to ensure that economies exit to a very different model of growth than that of the past 20 years. So far, there is little recognition of this in the international economic institutions, despite the fact that for the mainstream economics profession the crisis was the equivalent of the political scientists' "Berlin Wall moment" – i.e. nobody saw it coming.

> *It is imperative that the new policies are put in place to ensure that economies exit to a very different model of growth*

The IMF and OECD economists prepared a paper for the G8 in June 2009 on the medium-term policies. This is not a call for a return to "business as usual" once the crisis is over – from a labour perspective it is much worse, as it involves:

- drastic cutbacks in public expenditure to curb the accumulation of public debt, in part debt accumulated in bailing out the bankers;
- cutting back pension entitlements, notably those of public sector workers, in view of demographic changes;
- more regressive tax systems, cutting on corporate income tax and top personal income tax, while increasing taxes that hit working families front on, such as VAT; and

- wage flexibility, i.e. wage reductions and more labour deregulation in OECD countries to compete with a Chinese economy becoming more integrated into the global economy.

That is a profoundly unacceptable vision of the future. Rather, we have to use this crisis to move to a very different exit from the crisis, one that does not just get us out of the mess, but in which governments act together to create a new and different future:

- where growth is more balanced between North and South;
- where growth does not destroy the environment and is part of a carbon-free future;
- where global finance is downsized – including with an international tax on financial transactions – and the financial sector is restored to its legitimate role of financing real investment;
- where the public sector plays a key role and we have fair tax systems; and above all
- where the fruits of growth are distributed fairly within and between countries.

That vision will require a very different model of global growth than one that the IMF is likely to propose. In the Trade Union Advisory Committee to the OECD, we have established a task force jointly with the ITUC and EUTC to bring together trade union thinking on this new model of growth over the coming months. We will want to work with the Global Union Research Network (GURN) as a forum for testing our ideas and bringing in new thinking. No one can doubt the difficulties of shifting the paradigm thinking of the past 20 years – but we have to succeed: we cannot allow the victims of this crisis to be the ones who pay for it. We must come out of the crisis with strengthened economies, strengthened societies and a strengthened labour movement.

John Evans is General Secretary of the Paris-based Trade Union Advisory Committee (TUAC) to the OECD. Prior to joining TUAC, his previous appointments have included Research Officer at the European Trade Union Institute (ETUI) in Brussels, Industry Secretary at the International Federation of Commercial, Clerical and Technical Employees (FIET) in Geneva and Economist in the Economic Department of the Trades Union Congress (TUC) in London. He is currently a member of the Board of the Global Reporting Initiative, and member of the Helsinki Group.

Beyond "stimulus": Fiscal policy after the Great Recession

Andrew Jackson

As the communiqué from the Pittsburgh G20 summit put it, "it worked". Unprecedented macroeconomic stimulus in the form of ultra-low interest rates and large government deficits has pulled the global economy back from the abyss, at least for now. But what comes next? Conventional economic wisdom is setting the stage for deep and damaging cuts to public expenditures if labour and the progressive left do not win the argument for public investment-led growth and increased fiscal capacity.

Now is definitely not the time for a quick return to budget balance. Not only is the recovery very fragile, interest rates are likely to remain low. This means we can finance public expenditures which create jobs now while raising our productive potential and the future tax base. Debt incurred today to create a larger economy tomorrow is no burden on future generations.

> *Debt incurred today to create a larger economy tomorrow is no burden on future generations*

The International Monetary Fund, the OECD and most governments accept that stimulus should continue a bit longer while awaiting convincing evidence of a sustained revival of private sector demand. But spending cuts are clearly on the agenda. Citing the need to stabilize public debt in the context of rapidly ageing societies, the IMF recently (3 November 2009) painted a grim fiscal outlook for the advanced industrial countries, calculating that the primary budget balance (the surplus of revenues over programme expenditures) will have to be increased by a hefty 8 percentage points of GDP from 2010 levels to bring government debt down to a tolerable 60 per cent of GDP by 2030. The conventional view is that this move back to balanced budgets will have to come much more from deep cuts to public spending than from tax increases.

The dominant view is that both fiscal and monetary policy should tighten over what already promises to be a very sluggish recovery. That is a pretty dismal prospect. It translates into continued very high unemployment and substantial slack in the economy. Operating below capacity means low levels of public and private investment, which in turn lowers the potential for future growth. In human terms, an economy bumping along bottom means no jobs for young people, rising inequality and rising poverty. Moreover, fiscal retrenchment will translate into an unwelcome combination of public sector job cuts, cuts to public services and cuts to income support programmes, all of which are central to the well-being of working people.

Workers face the imminent prospect of paying for the economic crisis twice, first in the form of job and wage losses, and second in the form of cuts to the already inadequate public services and social programmes which existed in most countries before the recession.

While interest rates should remain low, there are major problems with any combination of fiscal austerity and loose monetary policy. Ultra-low interest rates and major injections of liquidity into the banking system are already fuelling new financial asset price bubbles. Led by major institutional investors, the shift back into equities and other assets has got well ahead of any recovery in the real economy. Meanwhile, low interest rates alone will not revive private sector demand. In most advanced industrial countries, especially in Canada, the United Kingdom and the United States, households are already deep in debt. Because of global over-capacity and unbalanced trade with Asia, real private sector investment in the advanced industrial countries is likely to remain very depressed. Thus fiscal austerity combined with monetary ease will not fix the underlying problem of stagnation.

One way out of this problem is to more closely control the credit process. We could and should be limiting highly leveraged financial investments and controlling unsustainable credit flows. The other way out of the problem is to run productive fiscal deficits to ensure that the impact of low interest rates is felt through higher public investment. It is desirable that the overall credit creation process should be driven by investment rather than by speculation and debt-financed consumption and, under today's circumstances, this requires high levels of public investment.

Now is the time to launch major medium and long term public investments to drive job creation, and also to create new investment opportunities for industrial sectors which remain in deep crisis. We must address long-standing investment deficits in basic municipal infrastructure; build new urban and intercity transportation systems; invest in energy conservation; dramatically expand non-carbon-based energy sources; expand basic public services such as not-for-profit childcare and elder care; and invest much more in public education at all levels as well as in workers' skills.

Well-selected investments can yield very high rates of return on a number of fronts. For example, investment in transit and passenger rail can have large positive job impacts, significantly cut carbon emissions, and also generate high rates of return to individuals and businesses in terms of reduced travel time and reduced road congestion. We know that all of these investments – especially those in public services and energy efficiency – are labour-intensive and create many more jobs than increased consumer spending, and simultaneously promote our environmental, community development and social justice goals.

What we need is a period of public investment-led growth to drive the whole economy. Good public infrastructure and good public services are key drivers of private sector productivity. Public sector investments drive investment by private sector suppliers, especially if twinned to coherent industrial strategies. The key point is that deficits can and should be incurred so long as they are twinned to public investment programmes which can be demonstrably linked to increasing overall economic potential and to furthering environmental and social goals. The challenge for labour and the left is to move from talking about temporary "stimulus" to promoting a pro-active, longer term public investment agenda.

> *Public sector investments drive investment by private sector suppliers, especially if twinned to coherent industrial strategies*

But how are we going to pay for major new public investments when deficits and debts are, supposedly, already too high? In the short term, low interest rates make viable a huge raft of potential public and environmental investments which will more than pay for themselves over time. In the longer term, a decade and more of expensive and wasteful tax cuts mainly in favour of corporations and those with very high incomes means that there is ample room to increase government fiscal capacity to balance budgets without cutting spending, and without undermining the living standards of working people.

Labour and the left have to recognize that decent levels of public services and social programmes ultimately have to be paid for from a high, comprehensive and fairly flat tax base including consumption and payroll taxes. If we want Scandinavian-type welfare states, we will have to pay Scandinavian-level taxes as a share of GDP. This reality is often ignored at our peril. In low-tax countries like Canada, the United Kingdom and the United States, we have to make the argument that we are all better off if we enhance fiscal capacity by raising money from a comprehensive tax system, and spending the proceeds on a broad array of equalizing public services and social programmes. We have to make the case for a shift from private consumption to public services and public investment, rather than pretend we can deficit finance permanent increments to the social wage.

To be sure, we also need to enhance the progressive elements of the overall tax system. We could and should gain useful amounts of revenue by levying higher rates of income tax on the very affluent. True, the rich are few in numbers, but they do have a high and rising share of personal income in most countries. This should be reduced by raising their taxes and redistributing the proceeds as equalizing transfers. Corporations could also pay more, though there is a case for redirecting higher corporate tax revenues into more effective ways of supporting real economy private investment rather than into general revenues. The G20 agenda should include coordinated upward harmonization of taxes on all forms of capital and on high incomes, as well as a financial transactions tax which would hit unproductive but highly profitable financial sector hyperactivity.

To conclude, we will soon be entering a major debate in most countries over the pros and cons of fiscal austerity. The right will argue that we need to cut quickly and deeply in the name of future generations. Our argument has to go beyond the need for temporary "stimulus". We must call for a deliberate strategy of public investment-led growth, and the gradual enhancement of fiscal capacity to pay for a more equal society.

Andrew Jackson is Chief Economist and National Director of Social and Economic Policy with the Canadian Labour Congress, where he has worked since 1989. He is also a research professor in the Institute of Political Economy at Carleton University, a research associate with the Canadian Centre for Policy Alternatives, and a fellow with the School of Policy Studies at Queen's University. He has written numerous articles for popular and academic publications, and is the author of Work and labour in Canada: Critical issues *(Canadian Scholars Press, 2005).*

Profits, banks and the state: How to get investment going again

Engelbert Stockhammer

The world is still experiencing the worst economic crisis since the 1930s. While the economic forecasts have brightened up recently, the overall picture is still gloomy. The collapse has been stopped, but the recovery is likely to be muted. This is for three reasons. First, US households, which have been the most dynamic source of demand in the past decade, are deeply in debt – and their houses, the biggest part of their wealth, are worth a lot less. Thus they are not likely to resume spending in the near future. Second, the banks are still in a lot of trouble. The big bank crash after Lehman Brothers has been avoided, but their balance sheets are still loaded with dubious assets and most make their money from trading, i.e. speculating, rather than from extending credit to businesses. It will be hard to get credit for a while. Third, government expenditures that have prevented the meltdown are being rolled back. After the panic of late 2008, normalcy has returned to economic policy-making. And in a neoliberal world it is considered normal that states have to balance their books, rather than help the economy or the poor. In short, while the worst is over, the bad is still to come. In particular, unemployment is still rising and will continue to do so.

So how could we get the economy going again? The key component of growth in a healthy economy is investment. Investment is an important source of demand, but it also provides the capital stock needed for future production. There are two types of investment: private and public. Private investment depends on business expectations about demand and profitability and on the availability of credit. Given the extent of the present crisis, it's unsurprising that businesses are reluctant to invest. Academic research has clearly identified demand as the single most important determinant of investment. Indeed, who would invest if they think they can't sell the output? The lesson for policy-makers is clear: stabilize demand or the private sector won't invest.

Obviously, capitalism is about making money, so firms are unlikely to invest unless they expect to make a profit. However, the importance of profits for investment is often overstated. Indeed, one of the great puzzles of the past decades is why firms (at least outside China) have not invested more, given their abundant profits. Looking at the United States and the European Union, in 1980 around two-thirds of profits were reinvested, while in 2007 only half were reinvested. Why don't firms invest when they are sitting on all this cash? The short answer is shareholder value orientation and globalization. Firms now distribute a lot more money to their shareholders through dividend payments or through share buy-backs. Firms are run to the benefit of shareholders. Globalization means that a lot of firms outsource production, reducing investment at home. This has mixed effects in the countries of the South and the East: it increases production there, but this is often in enclaves that are badly connected to the local economies and it often increases inequality.

> One of the great puzzles of the past decades is why firms have not invested more, given their abundant profits

The take-home from this is that the problem is not a lack of profits. Profits have been buoyant in the past without much investment taking place. Wage moderation will thus not help investment. Indeed, it will make matters worse. In particular, in countries with a large enough domestic market, such as Germany, wage moderation will depress domestic (consumption) demand further, creating an environment that is detrimental to investment. In a recent study (with Özlem Onaran and Stefan Ederer), we found that in Europe a redistribution of €1,000 from wages to profits will lead to about €100 more of investment, but to €350 less consumption (Stockhammer et al., 2009).

Access to credit is a more legitimate cause to worry about for businesses. Banks with problems on their balance sheets will be reluctant to lend. Monetary policy has so far helped to restore bank profitability, but has not been effective in ensuring that banks lend. Simply put, banks can earn a lot of money now, taking credit from the central banks and buying government bonds. There is no need to bother with old-fashioned business credit. Perversely, governments in many industrial countries now own substantial parts of the banks. But they are reluctant to interfere with their policy. Instead they have provided capital for the big banks in need and now watch how they are run in the interest of shareholders again.

All this may sound like there is little that governments can do to stimulate investment. But this is far from the truth. There is not only private but also public investment. In the 1930s, public investment projects were used on a massive scale to revitalize the economy. However, today there is great reluctance to do so. Indeed, the IMF and the OECD are eager to push governments to turn to a more restrictive policy. Now with the shock of the imminent collapse over, business is returning to normal – and this means a small state. As if nothing had happened in the past two years! Much of this approach is a legacy of the neoliberal domination that has preached the superiority of private investment over public activity. But the near-meltdown of the financial sector in 2008 should have made it clear that the private capitalist sector does not possess the miraculous properties of efficiency. Sure, governments often fall prey to corruption and may serve petty interests, but so does the private sector. Remember Bernard Madoff? Or Enron?

How should public investment be financed? Of course the largest demand effect will arise if government expenditures are credit financed. However, this will also increase public debt. If expenditures are financed by raising taxes, ways to do so in a progressive manner include closing tax havens and establishing wealth taxes and a financial transactions tax. All of these could raise substantial amounts without negative effects on demand. Closing overseas tax havens has been estimated to have the capacity to generate global additional revenues of US$100 billion (Cavanagh et al., 2009). A recent study found that a (worldwide) financial transactions tax of 0.1 per cent would raise about 1.5 per cent of world GDP (Schulmeister. Schratzenstaller and Picek, 2008).

If expenditures are financed by raising taxes, ways to do so in a progressive manner include closing tax havens and establishing wealth taxes and a financial transactions tax

Thus the pragmatic question should be whether there is a material need for investment projects in public infrastructure that the private sector is unlikely to provide. And the answer is a clear yes. From modernizing (or building) public transportation to investing in energy-saving technology and from spending on education to housing projects, there are plenty of areas where the social return to public investment is large enough to justify spending. Now is the time.

Further reading and references

Cavanagh, J. et al. 2009. "Reversing the great tax shift: Seven steps to finance our economic recovery fairly". Available at: http://www.ips-dc.org/getfile.php?id=356 [4 May 2010].

Jetin, B.; Denys, L. 2005. *Ready for implementation: Technical and legal aspects of a currency transaction tax and its implementation in the EU* (Berlin, WEED). Available at: http://www2.weed-online.org/uploads/CTT_Ready_for_Implementation.pdf [4 May 2010].

Pollin, R.; Heintz, J.; Garrett-Peltier, H. 2009. "The economic benefits of investing in clean energy: June 2009". Available at: http://www.americanprogress.org/issues/2009/06/pdf/peri_report.pdf [4 May 2010].

Schulmeister, S.; Schratzenstaller, M.; Picek, O. 2008. "A general financial transaction tax: Source of finance and enhancement of financial stability". Presentation at the European Parliament in Brussels on 16 April 2008. Available at: http://www.greens-efa.org/cms/default/dokbin/231/231075.a_general_financial_transaction_tax_sour@en.pdf [4 May 2010].

Stockhammer, E.; Onaran, Ö.; Ederer, S. 2009. "Functional income distribution and aggregate demand in the Euro area", in *Cambridge Journal of Economics*, Vol. 33, No. 1, pp. 139–159. The working paper version is available at: http://www.wu-wien.ac.at/inst/vw1/papers/wu-wp102.pdf [4 May 2010].

Engelbert Stockhammer works at the Kingston University, London. His research interests include macroeconomics, income distribution and financial systems. He recently authored The rise of unemployment in Europe *(Edward Elgar, 2004) and co-edited* Macroeconomic policies on shaky foundations: Whither mainstream economics? *(Metropolis, 2009).*

Why we should care about wages

Patrick Belser

A labour market view of the crisis

The past two years have witnessed the worst global economic recession since 1929. The financial crisis, which started in the United States and was triggered by a speculative bubble in the housing market, sent a shock wave through the real economy and labour markets around the world. The most immediate impact on labour markets has been the explosion of unemployment rates. In the United States, unemployment figures have exceeded the 10 per cent threshold in October 2009. The euro area is not far behind, with an average unemployment rate of 9.7 per cent in September 2009. In some European countries, the proportion of people looking for a job has reached dramatic proportions, with figures close to 20 per cent in both Latvia and Spain.

But that is not all there is. Focusing on unemployment rates alone understates the true extent of the deterioration of employment and conditions of work in labour markets. Everywhere, the crisis has led to cuts in working time, which has damaged the living standards of workers and their families. In the 27 Member States of the European Union, full-time employees work about three-quarters of an hour less every week than they did before the crisis. In the United States, weekly working time for production and non-supervisory workers has fallen by about half an hour. These average changes may seem relatively small because not everyone was affected; however, for those who were hit, the cuts in hours have often been severe. Similar trends have been observed elsewhere and, globally, the number of involuntary part-time workers appears to have increased.

Focusing on unemployment rates alone understates the true extent of the deterioration of employment and conditions of work

The result, in most cases, has been a fall in take-home pay for workers at the end of the month. Figures collected at the ILO for 53 countries show that in 2008 real monthly wages (i.e. wages adjusted for inflation) fell in one-quarter of all countries. In most other countries, particularly developing countries, wages continued to grow but at a much slower pace than before the crisis. The situation is likely to have been even worse in 2009, given the quarterly figures already available and the increase in the supply of unemployed people looking for jobs. Another worrying problem is the increase in the late-payment or non-payment of wages, particularly in transition economies such as the Russian Federation and Ukraine.

Wages and the recovery

Why should we care about wages, and not just unemployment? There are at least three reasons. The first has to do with social justice and the hardships that lower wages inflict on workers and their families, particularly at the lower end of the income distribution. In the United States, 7.5 million people work for earnings that fall below the poverty level and in Europe 8 per cent of workers can be called "working poor". For these workers even small changes in wages can represent large differences in living standards. Furthermore, the crisis comes after years of wage moderation and increasing inequality. Before the crisis, the wages of median and low-paid workers have remained largely flat despite considerable increases in economy-wide productivity. So one question is: where has the money gone? Research shows that high earners have benefited most, and that a large share of the rest has gone into corporate profits and investment.

The second reason why we should care is that a continued deterioration in wages is bad news for the economic recovery. The pace of the recovery depends largely on the extent to which people are able to consume whatever the global economy produces. And consumption, in turn, depends on the level of wages. In fact, in some advanced economies, almost 80 per cent of household income comes from wages and salaries. Although GDP figures in the course of 2009 provided indications of a possible economic rebound, the trends in real wages observed during the past few quarters raise serious questions about the true extent of a global economic recovery and also highlight the risks of phasing out government rescue packages too early. As the experience of Japan during the past decade has cruelly shown, wage deflation deprives national economies of much needed demand and can result in lengthy periods of economic stagnation.

Finally, we should already be thinking about the post-crisis world. Before the crisis, in the period from 1995 to 2007, the share of wages in GDP had declined in a majority of countries for which data is available. This may have been due to a combination of weaker trade unions, labour-saving technology, openness to trade and the pressures arising from the financial markets. Whatever the cause, the imbalance between increasing profits and stagnating wages has contributed to the crisis by creating an explosive mixture of high liquidity on financial markets, low rates of interest, and huge household debts. A system of bonuses which distorted incentives towards short-term risk provided the additional dynamite. For a more stable future, we should identify policies which ensure that productivity growth – when it is back – translates into adequate increases in wages for a majority, and not just higher bonuses for a few. Only this way can advanced economies achieve more sustainable patterns of consumption and investment.

Where to start?

The first immediate priority for governments in advanced economies has been to provide support to economic activity through large fiscal stimulus packages. Through this channel governments have provided some much needed demand for goods and services, which in turn has prevented a further decline in labour demand, employment and wages. Thanks to these measures, a social catastrophe has been avoided. For a sample of 19 OECD countries, the ILO estimates that fiscal stimulus packages have prevented between 3.2 million and 5.5 million additional job losses.

A majority of governments in OECD countries have taken additional measures to limit the damage inflicted by the crisis on employment and wages. One effective method has been the use of work-sharing arrangements, which have often combined shorter working times (to avoid layoffs) with wage subsidies. The latter have been provided through partial unemployment compensation or from general government revenues. According to the OECD, 22 out of 29 countries surveyed have put in place such a system. The most publicized example has been the case of Germany's *Kurzarbeit* (short work), which has benefited up to 1.5 million workers. Companies have also benefited from being able to keep their skilled workers on the payroll. Given the severity of the employment crisis, these temporary measures should not be phased out too early.

Worldwide, a considerable number of countries have also increased the purchasing power of low-paid workers through minimum wages. Figures collected by the ILO show that in 2008 half of 86 countries sampled have increased the minimum wage in real terms. A number of countries, including major economies such as Brazil, Japan, the Russian Federation and the United States, have pursued this policy in 2009. Minimum wages can have negative impacts on employment if they are set too high. However, the more recent literature shows that, when set at a level which takes into account the situation of workers and their families as well as productivity and other economic factors (as recommended in The Minimum Wage Fixing Convention, 1970 (No. 131)), minimum wages can increase the living standards of low-paid workers at little or no cost to aggregate employment. And for individual companies that are in such severe economic difficulties that they cannot even afford to pay minimum wages, there is always the possibility to provide smart exemptions or tax incentives, as is done in Indonesia for example.

But the deeper, more challenging need is to strengthen collective bargaining over wages. The ILO *Global Wage Report 2008/09* showed that when a large share of workers is covered by collective bargaining agreements the transmission mechanism between productivity and wages works pretty well: over the period 1995–2007 a 1 per cent increase in GDP per capita (an indicator of productivity growth) translated into an almost equal increase in wages. But where the coverage of collective bargaining is weak, the report calculated that each additional 1 per cent growth in GDP per capita only led to a 0.65 per cent increase in average wages. Thus, governments and social partners would be well advised to start consultations on how to strengthen constructive collective bargaining as part of a wider set of economic and industrial policies that can contribute to a fairer and more sustainable global economic recovery.

Further reading and references

ILO. *Global Wage Report 2008/09. Minimum wages and collective bargaining: Towards policy coherence* (Geneva).

ILO. *Global Wage Report, Update 2009*. Available at: http://www.ilo.org/public/english/protection/condtrav/index.htm [4 May 2010].

Patrick Belser is the principal editor of the ILO Global Wage Report. Before working on wages, he spent five years with the ILO programme on fundamental principles and rights at work and co-edited Forced labor: Coercion and exploitation in the private economy *(Lynne Rienner, 2009). He holds a Ph.D. from the Institute of Development Studies in Sussex. Before joining the ILO, he worked at the World Bank in Viet Nam and at the Swiss Secretariat for Economic Affairs in Berne.*

Putting employment security first will diminish demand: A warning from Germany

Heiner Flassbeck

The current global recession and fear of increasing redundancies has shifted the emphasis of the German labour movement from one concerning pay claims to one concerning employment security, which has become the name of the game. Even the metalworkers' union IG Metall is openly putting employment security before pay claims in their demands. Wage rises and hour cuts can be forgone, so long as not too many heads roll in the workplace.

I would like to argue that this emphasis is a serious mistake and that employment security achieved through wage restraint is likely to have negative effects across the economy and delay Germany's recovery from the recession. While wage restraint may preserve jobs within a firm, it has knock-on effects that will only serve to deepen the recession through their impact on demand. The current crisis brings into stark relief the failure of unions in Germany to examine seriously the impact of working-time reduction and the associated wage reduction, or lesser wage increases, on demand in the economy as a whole.

> *While wage restraint may preserve jobs within a firm, it has knock-on effects that will only serve to deepen the recession*

Take, for example, what has become a classic case. The Daimler company goes into the red. It agrees with the unions to make a 10 per cent uncompensated cut in the hours of those employees who are not already on short-time working arrangements. The positive trade-off is that there are no redundancies and Daimler's wage bill for the 90,000 employees affected is effectively reduced by 10 per cent. At an average monthly wage of €4,000, the firm saves more than €400 million. This represents a very significant reduction in Daimler's expected losses!

However, for the economy as a whole, the sums look rather different. Assuming that Daimler workers maintain relatively stable purchasing patterns, the €400 million saved by Daimler will reduce demand for other firms' products by the same amount as Daimler employees tighten their belts, so that the expected losses of other firms effectively increase by the same amount as the reduction in Daimler's expected losses. This simple example shows how the savings measures taken by one company and its unions do not spell out improvements at all, even at the outset. Furthermore, if other firms who bear an increased burden from the falling demand associated with Daimler's cutbacks follow suit, this could have a disastrous and far-reaching impact across the economy. Suppose the wages of the 10 million employees in all of Germany's industrial workplaces were reduced by 10 per cent over the course of the next year. Once again assuming that the employees' saving habits remained unaltered, this measure alone would cut demand across the economy by about €50 billion.

What are firms in general going to do when they notice that their loss predictions are systematically wrong, because demand is continually weaker than anticipated? Go back to the unions again in hopes of negotiating a 20 per cent reduction? Firms may also try to maintain their market share at a time of falling demand by passing on the cost reductions as price reductions. If only one firm does this, the situation of all the others will get even worse. If they all do it, prices may fall by so much that the workers will regain their previous purchasing power. So in real terms, they will be pocketing as much as before for working less. The outcome will then be not a cost reduction, but deflation. This is turn will lead to sluggish consumption, as people expect prices to drop even further in the near future.

So what are the unions to do? It has become a common perception that unions cannot go on making the same demands as they did prior to the crisis. I disagree and would argue that they can. In fact, campaigning for and winning wage increases in line with productivity gains could lead workers to act together to overcome this crisis quickly. The great majority of consumers in Germany are workers or pensioners. Only if they can expect their incomes to rise at the normal rate despite the crisis, i.e. in line with the medium-term productivity growth trend of around 1.5 per cent plus the European Central Bank's target inflation rate of 2 per cent, can Germany pull out of the crisis under its own steam.

Wage increases in line with productivity gains could lead workers to act together to overcome this crisis quickly

Such a campaign is likely to be met with strong objections as firms face shrinking profits and find themselves at overcapacity. It should however be remembered that many firms' profits skyrocketed in the years just before the crisis, particularly in the context of foreign trade. Nonetheless, the logic of macroeconomic theory suggests no alternative solution to the one outlined above if Germany wishes to recover from the crisis and attain a stable growth path in the not-too-distant future.

In contrast to previous experiences, hopes of export-led growth prompted by falling costs ring hollow this time around. The euro has already risen strongly. It would appreciate even further if the biggest national economy in the Eurozone staked everything on a foreign trade surplus, as it did from 2005 to 2008, thus relying on other countries shouldering new foreign debt. In addition, both consumption and investment are very weak in Europe and the United States, Eastern Europe is still in deep financial crisis, and the countries of Asia are themselves going all-out for export surpluses.

It follows that there is only one reliable way out of the crisis. The state must, once again, give the economy a boost by contracting even greater debts than already planned. This would enable firms to do the right thing in terms of wage-setting for the economy as a whole, and would be the most effective way of boosting demand and accelerating economic recovery. Tax cuts, as planned by the German Government, are not an appropriate way of achieving this. Some 15–20 per cent of the money will simply vanish into savings accounts, and the much-lauded "performance incentives" are simply a liberal pipe dream.

In contrast to debates in Germany, the issue of wage-induced consumption effects has been recognized in the United States. This is evident in the agressive deficit policy currently pursued by the US Government. In order to sidestep the wage reduction trap, into which a market economy will automatically fall without state involvement, the American deficit this year will be proportionately around three times bigger than the German one – about 12 per cent of GDP. The United States has learned from the experience of Japan, which for almost 20 years now has been unsuccessfully striving to escape from the deflationary wage policy that came into being after a great speculative bubble burst at the end of the 1980s. For Germany, the choices ahead are clear: either it will learn the Japanese lesson now, or it will have to learn it in face of stagnation and deflation later.

Heiner Flassbeck is currently Director of the Division on Globalization and Development Strategies of the United Nations Conference on Trade and Development (UNCTAD). He is the principal author and the leader of the team preparing UNCTAD's Trade and Development Report.

PART II

The need to reform global finance

Finance capital will not fade away on its own

Christoph Scherrer

With the fall of the investment bank Lehman Brothers in the late summer of 2008, many have predicted major reforms to reign in the hazardous behaviour of financial institutions. Nonetheless, up until very recently, little has happened. In early 2010, serious proposals for stricter oversight were considered for the first time. US President Barack Obama has proposed the most encompassing reform of the banking system – to prohibit bank holding companies from engaging in proprietary trading. This will allow them to purchase and sell stocks or derivatives only in the name of their clients. The purpose of the Volcker Rule – which Obama named after one of its strongest proponents, the former Federal Reserve chairman Paul Volcker – is to prevent banks (and possibly also the other largest financial institutions), as the central actors in the financial world, from bringing down the whole system through risky speculation.

Does Obama's proposal mark a change of course in favour of a more reasonable capitalism? The name alone casts doubts on the prospects of a much circumscribed financial sector. Volcker was the architect of the monetarist turn in central banking in the late 1970s, ushering in the period of neoliberalism. In the following, I will argue that the crisis alone will not lead to more labour-friendly policies. Crises are not only part of capitalism, they are also, as Karl Marx has pointed out, moments of capitalist reinvigoration. Crises delegitimize capitalists, but they also weaken their potential counter forces, especially organized labour.

Capitalist crisis solution

Marx would not have been too surprised about the course of the crisis so far. According to him, the destruction of capital is the main precondition for a new cycle of capital accumulation. The profits of the surviving capital will rise. In addition, the crisis speeds up innovation and leads to a higher degree of capital centralization as competitors are eliminated. More centralization promises higher profits because of increased economies of scale and market power. This theoretically stated mechanism of overcoming capitalist crisis seems to be empirically substantiated in the current crisis.

By turning away from the New Deal banking regulations, the United States experienced a rapid increase in bank concentration even before the crisis. This trend has continued. In 1995, the top five banks had 11 per cent deposit share. Their share increased to 29 per cent in 2004 and jumped to 38.6 per cent in 2009 (Celent, 2009). In the already highly concentrated banking market of Germany, only two of the five biggest private banks in 2006 survived in 2009. However, the crisis also brought forward new competition – mainly from the Far East. The competition, therefore, has reached a higher level.

> *In Germany, only two of the five biggest private banks in 2006 survived in 2009*

At the same time, the reputation of financial institutions has suffered badly. US taxpayers, in particular, have vented their anger at sizeable bonuses paid to those who effectively brought about the crisis. Will this spontaneous outrage lead to collective action? And if it does, what kind of action will follow? History informs us that the middle and working classes do not always direct their anger in dire economic times against the rich. They have also turned against members of their own class, and especially against poorer classes. In fact, electorally, many voters have turned Conservative in Europe since the outbreak of the crisis. While the election of Obama seems to contradict this trend, we are now witnessing the rise of a paranoid right in the United States. The newly emerging "Tea Party Movement" is turning its wrath against the federal government and Obama's slightly progressive policy proposals. They reckon that Washington has been captured by a finance-led cosmopolitan conspiracy.

The crisis weakens labour

In his essay in this book, Gregory Albo vividly describes the onslaught of capital on workers in North America. In order to understand the current weakness of labour, it might be helpful to look at the sources of worker power on a more abstract level. For the sake of simplification, four sources of power can be identified: market, associational, institutional and discursive power. The crisis undermines the market power of workers by letting demand for labour shrink. This also has an impact on its associational power. The export industries, the fortresses of organized labour in many countries, have suffered in the current crisis in particular. The well-organized and well-paid workers in the heavily impacted automobile industry are currently preoccupied by defensive struggles to keep "their" factories running. To a certain extent, their defence comes at the expense of the taxpayers and the so-called temporary workers, who have been dismissed in great numbers and without compensation (Brehmer and Seifert, 2009).

If workers relied solely on market and associational power, the fate of the majority of them would be left to the vagaries of the business cycle. On the basis of institutional power, they can secure their right to collective bargaining even during times of crisis. Their institutional power rests on their past organizational and political successes. The successes of US unions date back to an almost distant past and they command little institutional power at present. While they contributed to Obama's electoral success and the Democratic majority in Congress by mobilizing their members in large numbers, they failed to secure the support of the Democrats for their own top legislative priority, better legal protection for organizing (Greenhouse, 2009).

If workers relied solely on market and associational power, the fate of the majority of them would be left to the vagaries of the business cycle

Furthermore, organized labour usually lacks access to economic policy-making even when traditionally labour-friendly parties are in government. Leading representatives of such parties have supported the neoliberal agenda of the pre-crisis period. The financial centres of the United States have voted Democrats into office ever since 1992. Even in 2006, hedge funds supported Democrats by a margin of 3:1 over Republicans. It therefore came as no surprise that the Democratic senators Charles Schumer and Christopher Dodd defended finance capital during the crisis (Phillips, 2008). The German Social Democratic finance ministers in recent times, Hans Eichel and Peer Steinbrück, actively supported the liberalization of financial markets in the period before the crisis (Kellermann, 2005).

Thus, workers' organizations are left mainly with discursive power. Discursive power can be defined as the ability to convince others of one's own arguments. The crisis has delegitimized finance capital and its economic paradigm, neoliberalism, and therefore opens up space for alternatives. However, scandalizing the crisis is not sufficient for real change. A clear alternative to the status quo must be developed. Nevertheless, as yet, there has been little room for optimism.

It has become popular to point to the Great Depression as an example of the possibilities of changing course in the direction of a "good capitalism" (Dullien, Herr and Kellermann, 2009). What this analogy overlooks is that the shift towards welfare capitalism was not without alternatives (fascism and communism) and that it took the Second World War to decide which alternative to liberal capitalism would succeed. The parallel with the current situation is also flawed for other reasons. For one, learning from the Great Depression, today's policy-makers have acted against a deepening of the recession. The outcome so far is that the extent of the crisis and the level of social desperation cannot be compared to the 1930s in developed capitalist societies. Furthermore, it was precisely the existence of these alternatives to liberal capitalism that have led to its modification. Some social compromise was seen as the best defence of the private property order next to military might. These or other fundamental alternatives to liberalism are not currently in sight.

Change of course in the fourth year of the crisis?

President Obama's push for banking regulation is widely seen as a reaction to the increasing resentment among the US population about his closeness to Wall Street. His regulation proposal came on the heel of the election of a Republican candidate to succeed the deceased Democrat Edward Kennedy. Is a change of course therefore possible without a resurgent organized labour? Is the diffuse anger of the electorate sufficient? It is probably not. For one, it was not a socialist who became heir to Kennedy's Senate seat, but a proponent of free markets. In addition, Obama's proposal sounds a lot more radical than it is in reality. The prohibition of proprietary trading does not limit speculation in general; it only restricts the financial dealings of one group – the banks. Private investors would still be able to use hedge funds for risky deals with derivatives. They would still be allowed to take over companies for the purpose of selling them to other investors on the stock market after having them restructured, i.e. after having dismissed a significant part of their workforce. There would also be no limit for them to take on debt. Speculation with borrowed money drives bubbles and aggravates their subsequent implosion. Thus, Obama's proposal turns out to be a rather limited circumscription of the moneyed classes' sovereignty. Whether Obama will be able to pass even these timid reforms through Congress remains an open question. And as for the German Conservative Government, it lags way behind even Obama's tepid proposals.

In other words, we cannot expect the capitalists and their representatives to adopt a more reasonable course. We also have to recognize that the crisis weakens labour. Thus, what is to be done? The situation varies from country to country, but in general it is quite obvious that extraordinary efforts are called for. This begins with widespread support for workers who defend themselves against cuts in wages and jobs. Care should be taken that these do not come at the expense of weaker parts of the working class. The move from defensive to offensive strategies requires organized labour to become more political. Together with other social forces, it has to develop alternative visions and it has to regain influence in political parties.

References

Brehmer, W.; Siefert, H. 2009. "Sind atypische Beschäftigungsverhältnisse prekär? Eine empirische Analyse sozialer Risiken", in *Zeitschrift für Arbeitsmarktforschung*, Vol. 41 No. 4, pp. 501–531.

Celent. 2009. "Too big to bail? Bank concentration in the developed world". Available at: http://www.celent.com/124_2079.htm [12 Oct. 2009].

Dullien, S.; Herr, H.; Kellermann, C. 2009. "Der gute Kapitalismus ... und was sich dafür nach der Krise ändern müsste", Bielefeld, Transcript.

Greenhouse, S. 2009. "Democrats cut labor provision unions sought", in *The New York Times*, 17 July.

Kellermann, C. 2005. "Disentangling Deutschland AG", in Beck; Klobes; Scherrer (eds), *Surviving globalization? Perspectives for the German economic model* (Dordrecht, Springer), pp. 111–132.

Phillips, K. 2008. *Bad money: Reckless finance, failed politics, and the global crisis of american capitalism* (New York, Viking Penguin).

Christoph Scherrer is Professor of Globalization and Politics at the University of Kassel. He is also Executive Director of the International Center for Development and Decent Work and a member of the Steering Committee of the Global Labour University.

Taxing financial transactions: The right thing to do when you owe $600 billion a year and have lost control over global finance

Pierre Habbard

For those who had placed some hope in the G20 process to start re-regulating global finance the result, so far, has been utterly disappointing. Governments and central banks have been as eager to bail out the bankers and take on their "toxic assets" as they have been reluctant to move decisively on financial regulation. At every G20 Summit since the first one in November 2008 in Washington, we have been told that a revamped and enhanced Financial Stability Board (FSB), which would include the IMF, the OECD, the Bank for International Settlements (BIS) and other key financial organizations, would lead the way with concrete deliverables to bring the focus of global finance back to the real economy. We have seen instead a long series of reports on what went wrong and "high level" principles and "guidance", but with no teeth when it comes to enforcement. If anything, these reports reveal the extent to which supervisory authorities are exposed to a "significant lack of information" on "where risks actually lie" (FSB and IMF, 2009). They tell us that, two years into the crisis, the "current state of analysis limits the extent to which very precise guidance can be developed" (BIS, FSB and IMF, 2009) and that "considerable work remains" (SSG, 2009) in the areas of banks' internal controls and regulatory infrastructure.

At the G20 Summit in Pittsburgh (G20, 2009) in September 2009, however, some hope emerged that at last something tangible could be agreed upon in the near future. G20 leaders called on the IMF to undertake research to determine a "fair and substantial contribution" that the financial sector could make to pay "for any burdens associated with government interventions to repair the banking system". They further asked the IMF "to strengthen its capacity to help its members cope with financial volatility, reducing the economic disruption from sudden swings in capital flows". Read together, the two mandates were seen as an opening to an old policy issue that had been long neglected by governments and international financial institutions: the creation of a global financial transaction tax (FTT).

In its original proposal by James Tobin in the 1970s (TUAC, 1995), the economic justification for an FTT starts with the acknowledgement of the harmful effects of short-term speculation producing strong and persistent deviations of asset prices from their theoretical equilibrium levels. Such "overshooting" in prices lead to speculative bubbles over the long run. A measured and controlled increase in transaction costs implied by an FTT (from 0.02 per cent up to 0.5 per cent) would slow down trading activities so as to align capital flows with economic fundamentals and the real economy, while freeing up new sources of financing for global public goods. Since then, the FTT has been developed in different ways by economists and civil society groups, each putting different weight on the twin objectives of curbing financial speculation and freeing up new sources to finance global public goods. In fact, some proposals had such a strong focus on financing for development that in most cases they explicitly excluded the initial objective of Tobin to curb speculation, targeting a minimalist tax rate of 0.005 per cent to avoid "producing market distortions" (Hillman, Kapoor and Spratt, 2007) or "disrupting the market" (Schmidt, 2007).

> The FTT has been developed in different ways ... , each putting different weight on the twin objectives of curbing financial speculation and freeing up new sources to finance global public goods

Unlike in the pre-crisis literature, the FTT has now gained considerable traction, both as a financial stability instrument and as a solution for financing development. There is a strong case for this. Regarding financial stability, it would be hard to contest that at least part of the crisis we face today has been triggered by a speculative bubble in the derivatives markets and by global imbalances of current accounts between regions and within regions. As Stephan Schulmeister (2009) puts it, the size of the trading in derivative products is just much too big to be accounted for by its original purpose: to hedge against price volatility or credit default risk. On the revenue side, OECD Governments still have to deliver on their past commitments to finance global public goods, including the Millennium Development Goals, but also on "new" demands regarding climate change adaptation and mitigation measures for developing countries (the financing of which was a major contributory factor in the failure of the Copenhagen Summit). According to estimates by the Trade Union Advisory Committee to the OECD (TUAC, 2010), the global public good resource gap that would emerge would be in the range of $324–336 billion per year between 2012 and 2017 ($156 billion for financing climate change measures in developing countries, $168–180 billion for Official Development Assistance to reach 0.7 per cent of GNI).

To make matters worse, the very same OECD Governments are running budget deficits at unprecedented levels as a result of the global crisis, including the bailing out of the banking sector. According to the OECD, the size of the fiscal consolidation that would be needed in the period 2012–17 to bring deficits back to normal levels (below 2 per cent) is projected at $300–370 billion per year – on top of the above resource gap for public goods. Unsurprisingly, the OECD experts would want to fund this gap with cuts in public expenditure, "long overdue reforms" to public pensions and regressive tax reforms that would hit working people front on. In the absence of new tax revenues, such a fiscal scenario would have working families pay twice for the crisis: first through rising unemployment and falling incomes and second as a result of cuts in public and social services.

Against this background – "heavily indebted rich countries" whose supervisory authorities have lost control over global finance – then surely now is the time to take the FTT option seriously. This is what many unions have been campaigning for, together with social movements, as seen in recent initiatives in the United States, Europe and Asia. For its part, the TUAC has been working on a paper (TUAC, 2010) on the parameters of a FTT together with the ITUC. Based on recent contributions by Dean Baker (Baker et al., 2009), Stephan Schulmeister (2009) and Bruno Jetin (2009), the paper shows that an FTT could be designed with different rates per counterparty (large banks, other financial institutions including hedge funds, and non-financial corporations) and per market ("traditional" foreign exchange markets, exchange-traded derivatives, over-the-counter derivatives). Such a multi-tiered tax regime would help hit where it really hurts and target the counterparties (e.g. large banks and hedge funds) and transactions (e.g. derivative products) that are more prone to speculative trading than others. The revenues generated would be in the range of $200–600 billion per year if the tax were applied on a global scale.

Following the G20 summit in Pittsburgh, the IMF was quick to publicly dismiss the FTT (IMF, 2009) as an option to be considered in the commissioned report.[1] The sceptical reaction of the IMF is not surprising. Ever since 1995, when the Tobin tax became a "global issue", the IMF has not seriously considered the issue. The main objections are with the negative impact that the reduction in trading volume would have on price volatility and market liquidity. Other objections relate to the potential transfer of the added transactions cost to "middle class investors", the opportunities for tax avoidance or the more economic theory textbook argument that tax should apply to value added, not to transactions. Baker (2010) has published a solid set of responses to those criticisms, as has Schulmeister. Overall, the single most important aspect to keep in mind in considering the pros and cons of an FTT is the need to look at the *specific* problems associated with the FTT (in contrast to generic problems that would also be encountered by comparable regulatory options). The concerns of the IMF and OECD about feasibility clearly belong to the latter category: yes, implementing an FTT would be complicated, but would it be more complicated to implement than an alternative solution that would deliver comparable financial stability and global public good financing? On that, the IMF has argued for the creation of a "global banking insurance scheme" as an alternative to an FTT. However, the two instruments differ in terms of both revenues (which would not be available for public goods under an insurance scheme) and the handling of risk. Regarding the latter, the insurance scheme in fact would be more onerous for regulators than the FTT. A prerequisite for any insurance scheme is the ability to price the risk associated with the banks' balance sheets, which in turn presupposes the ability of the insurer (the regulator) to conduct proper risk assessment of the insured (the banks) and to do so at reasonable costs. And yet it appears that such a basic requirement has become a step too far for financial authorities.

> An FTT would be complicated, but would it be more complicated ... than an alternative solution [delivering] comparable financial stability?

An FTT, unlike the insurance proposal, would provide governments with a powerful regulatory tool which would not depend on the ability of the supervisory authorities to price or assess risk. It would be no panacea for the much broader agenda on financial re-regulation, but it would offer government a "low-cost" instrument for tackling volatility in asset prices and for downsizing the global banking industry, particularly at a time when the international financial supervisory framework is in tatters and will take a decade to reform. It would free up new sources of financing for global public goods at a time when public services and welfare are at threat.

Note

[1] The IMF report, which was meant to remain confidential, was made public by the BBC on 20 April 2010 and can be accessed at: http://news.bbc.co.uk/2/shared/bsp/hi/pdfs/2010_04_20_imf_g20_interim_report.pdf

References

Baker, D. 2010. "Responses to criticisms of taxes on financial speculation", Center for Economic and Policy Research, University of Massachusetts, January 2010. Available at: http://www.cepr.net/documents/publications/ftt-criticisms-2010-01.pdf [4 May 2010].

Baker, D. et al. 2009. "The potential revenue from financial transactions taxes", Center for Economic and Policy Research and Political Economy Research Institute, University of Massachusetts, December 2009. Available at: http://www.cepr.net/documents/publications/ftt-revenue-2009-12.pdf [4 May 2010].

BIS; FSB; IMF. 2009. "Guidance to assess the systemic importance of financial institutions, markets and instruments: Initial considerations", Report to G20 Finance Ministers and Governors, September 2009. Available at: http://www.financialstabilityboard.org/publications/r_091107c.pdf [4 May 2010].

FSB; IMF. 2009. "The financial crisis and information gaps", Report to G20 Finance Ministers and Governors, September 2009. Available at: http://www.financialstabilityboard.org/publications/r_091107e.pdf [4 May 2010].

G20. 2009. "G20 Pittsburgh Summit leaders statement", 25 September 2009. Available at: http://www.g20.org/Documents/pittsburgh_summit_leaders_statement_250909.pdf [4 May 2010].

Hillman, D.; Kapoor, S.; Spratt, S. 2007. *Taking the next step – Implementing a currency transaction development levy*, Report commissioned by the Norwegian Ministry of Foreign Affairs, February 2007. Available at: http://mpra.ub.uni-muenchen.de/4054/1/MPRA_paper_4054.pdf [4 May 2010].

IMF. 2009. Transcript of a Press Conference by IMF Managing Director Dominique Strauss-Kahn with First Deputy Managing Director John Lipsky and External Relations Director Caroline Atkinson, Istanbul, 2 October 2009. Available at: http://www.imf.org/external/np/tr/2009/tr100209.htm [4 May 2010].

Jetin, B. 2009. "Financing development with global taxes: Fiscal revenues of a currency transaction tax", Université Paris-Nord, March 2009. Available at: http://gesd.free.fr/jetin39.pdf [4 May 2010].

Schmidt, R. 2007. "The currency transaction tax: Rate and revenue estimates", The North–South Institute (Canada), October 2007. Available at: http://www.nsi-ins.ca/english/pdf/CTT%20revenue.pdf [4 May 2010].

Schulmeister, S. 2009. "A general financial transaction tax: A short cut of the pros, the cons and a proposal", Österreichisches Institut für Wirtschaftsforschung (WIFO), September 2009. Available at: http://www.wifo.ac.at/wwa/servlet/wwa.upload.DownloadServlet/bdoc/WP_2009_344$.PDF [4 May 2010].

SSG. 2009. "Risk management lessons from the global banking crisis of 2008", Senior Supervisors Group, 21 October 2009. Available at: http://www.financialstabilityboard.org/publications/r_0910a.pdf [4 May 2010].

TUAC. 1995. Report on a TUAC–Canadian Labour Congress Round Table Discussion with James Tobin. TUAC, May 1995. Available at: http://www.tuac.org/en/public/e-docs/00/00/05/B0/document_doc.phtml [4 May 2010].

TUAC. 2010. "The parameters of a financial transaction tax and the OECD global public good resource gap, 2010–2020", TUAC Secretariat, 15 February 2010 Available at: http://www.tuac.org/en/public/e-docs/00/00/06/7C/document_doc.phtml [4 May 2010].

Pierre Habbard is Senior Policy Adviser, Trade Union Advisory Committee (TUAC) to the OECD.

Global Financial Crisis 2.0

Raymond Torres

Recovery prospects are being seriously hampered as a result of risk of a return to pre-crisis policy settings. By the end of 2009, the world economy was slowly recovering, aided by stimulus measures implemented by governments since the onset of the crisis. However, recent pressures for a return to orthodox policies in the context of an unreformed financial system threaten these fragile achievements.

The crisis led to a significant policy response by governments and monetary authorities. In advanced countries, interest rates were drastically reduced and have been maintained at a low level. Massive rescue packages to avoid a collapse of financial institutions were implemented – mainly in developed countries. And most countries that had a budget space implemented fiscal stimulus measures in the form of discretionary tax cuts, higher government spending or a combination of both. These fiscal measures were crucial to reviving the economy given the weakness of monetary policy tools in a context of "deleveraging" in the private sector and among financial institutions. According to ILO estimates, the fiscal stimulus measures amounted to around 1.7 per cent of world GDP.[1]

Overall, the measures have succeeded not only in supporting the economy but also in avoiding further significant job losses. Estimates are for an increase in world unemployment by over 20 million workers between the autumn of 2008 and the third quarter of 2009 for the 51 countries for which data are available.[2] This is less than what had been feared at the start of the crisis.[3] For instance, in European Union countries, the employment effects of falling GDP have been much less than was the case in earlier recessions.

This relatively favourable outcome reflects, first, the rapidity of the policy response. Research shows that, by adopting stimulus measures soon after the start of the crisis, countries could expect a significant positive impact on employment by mid-2010.[4] By contrast, a postponement of the measures by three months would delay employment recovery by six months – illustrating the disproportionate costs of inaction for employment.

Second, the fall in employment has been cushioned by the nature of the policy response itself, consistent with the ILO's Global Jobs Pact:[5]

- In the majority of cases, crisis responses have focused on stimulating aggregate demand. In particular, an effort has been made to enhance social protection (e.g. in Brazil and India), extend unemployment benefits (e.g. in Japan and the United States), to avoid cuts in minimum wages and to adopt other measures for low-income groups. These interventions, by sustaining the purchasing power of low-income groups, have effectively boosted aggregate demand while alleviating somewhat the social costs of the crisis.

- In countries like France, Germany and the Netherlands, short-time working arrangements have been aided by government subsidies. In other countries like Australia and the United States, part-time employment has surged. These policies have helped reduce job losses. In the face of growing credit constraints, an effort has been made to support otherwise sustainable enterprises (e.g. in the Republic of Korea).

- Finally, in the face of growing long-term unemployment, an effort has been made to enhance active labour market policies.

Recourse to inward-looking solutions has been limited so far. A generalized use of protectionist measures has been avoided, thereby reducing the risk of a collapse of international trade and investment, which could have a detrimental impact on developing countries. Importantly, there was a risk that countries would engage in a spiral of wage cuts and worker rights curtailing in order to improve competitiveness. This would have been a self-defeating and indeed counter-productive policy, given the global nature of the crisis and the need for greater aggregate demand. In addition, attempts to make workers pay for a crisis which originated in the financial system and was preceded by a significant increase in income inequalities and falling wage shares would have reduced public support for recovery packages.

Attempts to make workers pay for [the] crisis ... would have reduced public support for recovery packages

In short, the global policy response has succeeded in kick-starting an economic rebound and the policy response had also succeeded in attenuating job losses.

Unfortunately, the policy response did not tackle the key factor behind the crisis, namely a dysfunctional financial system. The result is, first, that the practices that developed before the crisis will inevitably re-emerge unless action is taken. In particular, a large share of the increase in profits has accrued to the financial sector – the financial sector's share of total corporate profit reached 42 per cent before the crisis, up from about 25 per cent in the early 1980s. And the profits of non-financial firms serve to pay dividends rather than invest in the real economy. During the 2000s, less than 40 per cent of profits of non-financial firms in developed countries were used to invest in physical capacity, which is 8 percentage points lower than during the early 1980s. Ever-growing pressures for more and better returns have adversely affected wages and job stability in the real economy.

Second, the lack of financial reform is reducing the room for pursuing the job-centred stimulus measures. Indeed, insufficiently regulated financial systems make it more difficult to channel credit to the real economy – so, other things equal, the amount of fiscal stimulus needed to achieve economic recovery is greater than in the presence of a well-functioning financial system.

At the same time, insufficiently regulated financial systems tend to penalize governments that run larger fiscal deficits. As a result, there is a growing risk that governments will prematurely remove the fiscal stimulus measures that helped avoid a deeper recession. Governments may feel they have to reduce quickly fiscal deficits in order to appear as credible as possible in the eyes of the financial markets and to reduce the risk of speculative attacks. This is illustrated by recent events in the Euro area: even countries with much lower public debts than Greece have had to adopt in haste fiscal packages that reassure markets. Importantly, an unpublished study by Reinhart and Rogoff on "growth in a time of debt" suggests that such moves lack economic foundation in countries where public debt is significantly lower than 90 per cent of GDP.

In addition, the type of fiscal restriction measures which are presently being considered tend to focus on spending cuts, in particular in the area of social policy, rather than on higher government revenues (including through vigorous campaign against tax competition and tax fraud, and consideration of new revenue sources such as green taxes). The risk is that welfare benefits – which proved so essential to ensuring adequate income support to the innocent victims of the crisis – will be cut. This would erode political support for the crisis response strategy, possibly leading to social unrest. In addition, by scaling back certain programmes, many jobseekers will be pushed out of the labour market, depriving the economy of valuable resources. Keeping well-designed programmes is in fact cheaper over the long term, given the favourable effects of these programmes on participation and skills.

Fiscal measures are still needed because the real economy is too weak to have gained an autonomous growth momentum, at least in developed countries where the process of "deleveraging" is far from finished.

In addition, countries also tend to move quickly to export-oriented strategies in order to improve the current account balance and to build up foreign exchange reserves, thus reducing perceived risks for financial operators. The problem is that some countries have to import in order for others to export – and the United States cannot remain the importer of last resort. Therefore, a quick return to export strategies would end up reducing the prospects for world trade and economic growth.

Altogether, we may be entering a new stage of the crisis where financial markets are adding pressure for an early exit from fiscal stimulus measures and for cuts in social protection and wages. This would strongly affect the world economy given the weak autonomous growth capacity of the private sector, which is partly due to continuously tight access to bank credit. It would also further prolong the employment recovery and erode social support for governments' crisis strategies.

Rescue packages to financial institutions have reached unprecedented levels in the countries where the crisis originated. The bill will be expensive for taxpayers and job losers. It is therefore essential to ensure that an end is put to those financial practices and irresponsible risk-taking that preceded the crisis. As noted by the Bank for International Settlements in its 2009 annual report, "A healthy financial system is a precondition for sustained recovery. Delaying financial repair risks hampering the efforts on other policy fronts."

True, the financial industry has undertaken steps to modify its practices through the adoption of codes of conduct and other non-binding initiatives. But there is concern that new regulations will push the financial industry to other locations. The overall impression is that, unless action is taken soon, business-as-usual will prevail. In such an unreformed context, the practices that provoked the financial crisis will resume soon after economic recovery starts. The pressures would aggravate the situation in a deteriorated world of work, while raising the risk of later crises.

Unless action is taken soon, ... the practices that provoked the financial crisis will resume

There are various options that can be considered in this respect. What is important is to address the root problems, in particular

- inadequate and incomplete regulation, and

- inappropriate incentives for risk-taking and pay of bank executives and traders.

For the reasons outlined above, the approach should be as coordinated as possible – at least at the level of the G20. Otherwise, free-riding problems will inevitably arise. This, together with proper implementation of the Global Jobs Pact, will support economic recovery in the short run, while paving the way for a more sustainable world economy.

Notes

[1] ILO: *The financial and economic crisis: A decent work response* (Geneva, 2009).

[2] International Institute for Labour Studies, *World of Work Report 2009: The global jobs crisis and beyond* (Geneva, 2009).

[3] ILO: *Global Employment Trends* (Geneva, 2010).

[4] ILO: *The financial and economic crisis* (Geneva, 2009).

[5] ILO: *Recovering from the crisis: A Global Jobs Pact* (Geneva, 2009).

Raymond Torres is Director for the International Institute for Labour Studies at the ILO. He recently launched the World of Work Report, *the new annual flagship publication from the Institute.*

The end of an era: What comes after financialization and what will be the consequences for labour?

Ekkehard Ernst

The global financial crisis that started in 2007 is marking the end of an era. This era has been characterized by deepening financial markets, a growth process driven by the accumulation of household debt and the international financial dominance of the North. The disruption of financial markets and the shake-up of the world trading system, however, are likely to undermine this economic model permanently. As a result of the crisis, new regulation may be introduced, political and economic power is likely to shift from North to South and new actors will be entering the scene. Most importantly, the legitimacy of earlier policy prescriptions which have led to a rising trend in social inequality[1] has been significantly undermined. Will this ring in a new high era for labour, as during the Fordist period? Or, by contrast, will distributional battles intensify? What will be the new sources of growth and who might benefit from them most? The jury is still out, as we are in the middle of the storm, but some new trends are already emerging that will shape the future ground for global governance.

> *The legitimacy of earlier policy prescriptions ... has been significantly undermined*

To understand the dynamics of the recovery and get a better grasp on different exit strategies from the crisis, it is useful to widen the scope and take a politico-economical perspective. The main actors are financial investors and their lobby groups, employers and employers' associations, and workers and trade unions. In the post-war era, with its large companies and relatively uncontested markets, benefits from growth were shared between employers and labour, often at the expense of investors. This changed when power shifted to investors during the era of financialization as a result of freer international capital flows and more open goods markets, and led to an erosion of labour's bargaining power.[2] Some of the factors that triggered that shift are still at work today. What has changed, however, is the legitimacy with which the community of financial investors has argued in the past for less stringent regulation and freer international capital flows. The crisis has undermined this position even in the eyes of the most favourable observer, and this may result in a rebalancing of power and a sharing of future benefits from growth.[3]

Shifting power will be shaping the crisis exit and recovery on two levels over the coming years. At a first, immediate, level, governments and lobby groups will clash over how best to regulate financial markets in order to restore some sense of medium-term stability. This may imply stricter rules for banks, requiring them to hold larger stocks of regulatory capital or to pay additional taxes to fund a government-sponsored financial safety net. It may also entail new rules to curb international capital flows, in particular the more volatile, short-term speculation with respect to currency markets, and to limit or prohibit the use of certain types of financial products deemed particularly dangerous for the stability of the system. Quite naturally, the banking industry and financial sector lobby groups are resisting any attempts at such regulation or are making only minimal concessions. The absence of a single international coordinating body that could produce a new international regulatory framework – the Bank for International Settlements is only a voluntary body and the International Monetary Fund does not have a mandate broad enough to cover all of these aspects – helps such lobby groups to limit governments in their regulatory ambitions. In addition, governments are increasingly constrained by the financial markets in their quest for new financial sources to fund their rising public debt. Even though deficit ratios are likely to go down with the economic recovery, existing debt has almost doubled in size in some countries and will need to be (re)financed in the future, creating favourable margins for political lobbying by financial investors.

At a second, more remote, level, different actors will strive for new sources of growth. Such a trend was already visible before the global crisis, as several larger economies showed signs of exhausting earlier productivity gains. The debt-driven recovery during the 2000s was temporarily hiding these structural problems, but is unlikely to be an acceptable or feasible source of growth in the future. New growth patterns require investment, however, and different views on what constitutes sustainable long-term growth will compete for scarce funds. One particular fault line will be whether these new growth drivers must be sought domestically or internationally, intensifying the use of export-led strategies. Clearly, a more sustainable long-term recovery of the world economy would require a stronger balance between domestic and foreign sources of growth. Strong interest groups, however,

> A more sustainable long-term recovery of the world economy would require a stronger balance between domestic and foreign sources of growth

particularly in those countries heavily reliant on external demand, have already started to push for policies to restore (price) competitiveness for faster export growth. Strengthening domestic sources of growth, on the other hand, would require reorienting private and public investment towards new sectors, such as environmentally related industries ("the green economy") or care services. To be fair, both sources – domestic and international – are not incompatible, but the coming regulatory changes – especially regarding international financial transactions – will have implications for their relative importance in the recovery and over the medium term.

What does this mean for labour? Will employment recover to previous levels? Can labour markets provide sufficient jobs to absorb an increasing world labour force? And under which conditions can this be achieved? The different forces that are shaping the path to recovery from the crisis give rise to four scenarios that are conceivable on the basis of these two lines of conflict:

- In the first scenario, finance wins on both accounts: financial regulation will be minimal and international capital markets will remain wide open. Governments will be constrained by their lack of additional funding, making any attempt at reorienting the growth process towards new, more sustainable sources difficult if not impossible. In this scenario, job volatility will remain high and employment growth may recover to earlier rates, but with the heightened risk of new periods of financial instability and crashes.

- In a second scenario, finance dominates the regulatory process, but sources of growth will be sought domestically. This may happen when protectionist reactions take over during the recovery phase. World trade will not return to earlier rates of expansion and global growth may remain below pre-crisis rates. In this scenario, employment may lose out on two grounds: economic dynamics will be lower and – due to the financial markets' dominance domestically – job volatility will remain high.

- A third outcome might be that financial market regulation stiffens substantially, but that international market openness continues. Such financial regulation could follow today's best practice countries (e.g. Canada), and banks might be required to hold higher reserve margins or to participate in a country-wide stabilization fund. Markets for goods and (financial) services would remain open, but the more restricted financial sector activity at home and the domestic quest for new sectors of growth will improve the bargaining power of workers and create new opportunities for employment. Destruction of jobs in declining industry may remain high, but so will job creation in new sectors. In this scenario, transitory job and worker flows are likely to be large and governments will need to make sure that they put policies in place to help the process.

- A final scenario might be that governments manage to impose a search for new domestic growth drivers. World trade is gradually being scaled down both as the result of a more restrictive international financial regime and due to – possibly environmentally related – tariff barriers. Bargaining power would shift back to labour, employment creation would intensify and profits would be shared more directly between firms and their workforces, instead of being distributed to financial investors.

We are at the beginning of this process and it can only be considered a Herculean task to evaluate the likelihood of any of these scenarios. Being aware of them, however, can shape current and future policy debates, so as to make sure that only those outcomes might be sought that promise the highest benefits to the real economy and ultimately translate into more and better jobs. What is emerging from these four scenarios is that domestic financial sector regulation is key for governments in terms of shaping the process of future growth. Even in the absence of international coordination, governments can gain the upper hand through carefully managed regulatory changes that reorient financial sector activities to support the real economy.

Notes

[1] *World of Work Report 2008: Income inequalities in the age of financial globalization* (Geneva, International Institute for Labour Studies/ILO).

[2] On this, see M. Pagano and P. Volpin: "The political economy of corporate governance", *American Economic Review* (2005), Vol. 95, No. 4, pp. 1005–1030, and M. Pagano and P. Volpin: "Workers, managers, and corporate control", in *Journal of Finance* (2005), Vol. 60, No. 2, pp. 841–868.

[3] A striking example of this was the Congressional testimony of former Fed Chairman Alan Greenspan on 23 October 2008: "The crisis however has turned out to be much broader than anything I could have imagined."

Ekkehard Ernst is Senior Economist at the International Institute for Labour Studies. He previously worked at the OECD and the European Central Bank. His work focuses on the interaction of financial and labour market dynamics.

PART III

The economic crisis and challenges to national policies

The international economic crisis and development strategy: A view from South Africa

Neva Seidman Makgetla

South Africa has been harshly affected by the international economic crisis, which led to a fall in the GDP and an even sharper contraction in employment. While job losses levelled out in the last quarter of 2009, the crisis will continue to shape long-run development. In particular, it points to the need for a development strategy that builds more on domestic and regional demand and that focuses explicitly on employment creation as central to a cohesive and equitable society.

South Africa's GDP declined by approximately 3 per cent between the last quarter of 2008 and the second quarter of 2009, and then increased in the third quarter of 2009. In comparison, the fall in employment proved steeper and more prolonged. The economy lost around a million jobs, or 6 per cent, between the fourth quarter of 2008 and the third quarter of 2009, and gained only 90,000 back in the last quarter of 2009.

The loss of employment took place in a context of extremely high joblessness. South Africa has long ranked as one of the ten countries with the lowest employment levels in the world. Less than half of all working-age adults earn an income, and the unemployment rate has been over 20 per cent since the Government began measuring it with the transition to democracy 15 years ago.

> South Africa has long ranked as one of the ten countries with the lowest employment levels in the world

The employment losses following from the global crisis aggravated the deep inequalities that have long characterized the South African economy. They had the heaviest impact on low-income workers, especially in marginalized sectors like informal, domestic and agricultural work. In addition, very high levels of job loss amongst young workers had particularly negative implications for social cohesion and long-term development.

The Government's short-run response included a countercyclical fiscal policy and substantial infrastructure investment. This response moderated the drop in investment and growth and presumably the loss of jobs. Still, the employment loss remained very large, and the Government's response did not provide direct support to the self-employed informal and domestic workers who lost their incomes. Nor did it address the rapid recovery in capital inflows, which as discussed below led to a stronger rand, making the economy as a whole less competitive.

The international crisis was associated with far-reaching structural changes in the global economy. That, in turn, has implications for South Africa's longer term development strategy. In particular, profound shifts in international markets make it seem even less likely that South Africa can in future grow on the basis of manufactured exports – the traditional approach to industrial policy that has been at the centre of the Government's economic strategy since the end of apartheid in 1994.

The emphasis on exporting manufactured goods has largely shaped the discourse on industrial policy worldwide as well as in South Africa.[1] It reflects the belief that the rapid economic growth in East Asia from the 1960s was rooted in vigorous industrial policies to support manufacturing for markets mostly in Europe and the United States.

Even before the crisis, this analysis of East Asian industrialization neglected three factors that enabled effective industrial policy there – and that were noticeably absent for South Africa:

1. East Asian countries generally enjoyed relative equality and social cohesion.[2] which meant both capital and workers were more likely to agree on economic growth as a social panacea. In particular, measures to raise productivity prove more acceptable in economies with high levels of low-wage employment than in economies with low employment, where growth through rising productivity in export sectors may be associated with very limited employment creation.

2. The United States provided extraordinary levels of support to the East Asian countries, which it saw at least until the 1990s as a bulwark against communism.

3. Over the past half-century East Asia as a whole gradually developed logistics and market systems that vastly reduced the cost of exporting to and communicating with the global North.

The international economic crisis laid bare a fourth obstacle to a growth strategy based on manufactured exports. That strategy explicitly assumed virtually unlimited demand in the global North, particularly in the United

States. It required that if countries could produce competitively, their sales would be assured.

Yet the downturn of the late 2000s could be understood as a crisis of inadequate demand. On the one hand, it resulted from deepening inequalities in much of the global North, offset in part by excessive household borrowing. On the other, it reflected the suppression of wages to support continued exports in much of East Asia, including China, as well as some European countries.

The growing global imbalance in demand that underpinned the boom of the 2000s was reflected in the huge balance of payments surpluses enjoyed by the rapidly growing economies of East Asia. The recycling of those surpluses laid the basis for the credit bubble that led to the financial crisis of late 2008. Once the credit bubble burst, demand for imports by the global North contracted sharply.

The prospects for resuming export-led growth remained unclear at the end of 2009. While economic expansion resumed in China and other Asian economies, exports remained far below the levels of 2008. To replace foreign demand, these countries embarked on extensive programmes to stimulate domestic sales, including subsidies for purchasers of consumer durables as well as massive investments in infrastructure.

These developments had significant implications for the prospects of South Africa and other resource-based economies in the global South. South Africa participated in the boom of the mid-2000s essentially by exporting mining products to world markets. The relatively strong rand of this period, based primarily on huge short-run capital inflows, largely blocked manufactured exports. While the economy continued to depend mostly on mining-based exports, employment growth occurred mostly in the services and construction, essentially to meet the needs of the small high-income group and state infrastructure and redistributive programmes.

The international economic downturn meant that South African efforts to expand exports of consumer and capital goods faced even steeper obstacles than during the boom. To start with, demand was suppressed in the global North. But the inflow of short-term capital resumed nonetheless, apparently largely due to measures to enhance liquidity in industrialized economies. South Africa saw an inflow of almost US$6 billion in the third quarter of 2009 alone. As a result, in real terms the rand strengthened to values last seen in 2004.

This situation called into question the basic thrust of South Africa's industrialization policy. For most of the period from 1994, whether implicitly or explicitly, the Government's industrial policy centred on supporting manufactured exports. It contained virtually no projects to meet domestic or regional demand or to create employment while raising living standards. The auto industry enjoyed by far the largest subsidies of any industry, with tax relief used mostly to encourage exports.[3] In contrast, the more broad-based Reconstruction and Development Programme (RDP) adopted by the African National Congress before coming into power expected housing construction and provision of government services to prove central to driving economic growth as well as improved welfare.[4]

In the event, the conventional industrial policy pursued from the mid-1990s proved singularly ineffective. In part, that reflected inadequate resourcing and inconsistent implementation. The share of total government spending going explicitly to support agriculture, mining, manufacturing and construction fell from 4 per cent in the mid-1990s to 3 per cent in the mid-2000s.[5] Moreover, the failure to limit short-run capital inflows and the consequent appreciation in the rand outweighed the limited policy support to manufacturing outside of autos. In these circumstances, exports from the mining value chain, including refined but not fabricated base metals, continued to contribute over half of all South African exports.

The global structural problems laid bare by the economic crisis point to the need for more innovative approaches to development. For South Africa, a viable growth strategy should focus on meeting needs in the domestic and regional markets, including basic consumer goods and infrastructure effectively funded through the state. In addition, it would need stronger measures to enhance the overall efficiency and inclusiveness of the economy by continuing to improve core economic infrastructure; addressing the serious problems with general education systems serving most black communities; and reducing the cost of living for working people, especially for food, public transport and health care. Finally, it should include institutional changes to mobilize domestic resources to fund priority investments while reducing dependence on short-run inflows of financing through the stock and bond markets.

A viable growth strategy should focus on meeting needs in the domestic and regional markets

This relatively modest growth strategy might seem second-best to establishing a world-class modern industrial economy. Given the emerging constraints on global demand, however, it is more likely to succeed in laying the basis for sustained growth than a classical export-oriented industrial strategy. Moreover, it would do more to generate opportunities for the majority of southern Africans in the short to medium term, helping to overcome the employment backlogs that the international economic crisis aggravated.

Notes

[1] See DTI: *Industrial Policy Action Plan (IPAP)* (Pretoria, DTI, 2007); as well as R. Hausman et al.: *Final recommendations of the International Panel on ASGISA*. (Pretoria, National Treasury, 2007).

[2] J.E. Campos and H. Root: *The key to the Asian miracle: Making shared growth credible* (Washington DC, The Brookings Institution, 1996).

[3] P. Barbour: *An assessment of South Africa's investment incentive regime with a focus on the manufacturing sector*, ESAU Working Paper 14 (London, ODI, 2005).

[4] ANC: *The Reconstruction and Development Programme: A policy framework* (Johannesburg: Umanyano Publications, 1994).

[5] Data on expenditure by sector from 1995 provided by the South African National Treasury in 2008.

Neva Makgetla is Lead Economist at the Development Bank of Southern Africa (DBSA). She has previously worked for COSATU and the South African Government.

The global footloose proletariat and the financial crisis: Reflections on the contradictions of export-oriented industrialization in India

Alessandra Mezzadri

Over three decades of neoliberal policies have had a severe effect on labour in developed and developing regions alike. In developed regions, neoliberalism managed to crush the resistance of organized labour, significantly curtailing its institutionalized power and splintering the "industrial citizenship" that characterized the Keynesian era. As increasing shares of manufacturing production migrated towards developing regions, where the development paradigm increasingly turned towards export-oriented strategies, armies of sweated labour were recruited to be deployed in the context of transnationalized production regimes.

The logic of export-oriented industrialization has been ferocious with labour in the so-called Global South. Simply reconceptualized as "comparative advantage", here labour has been exposed to harsh patterns of commodification. As illustrated in many empirical studies focusing on global production networks, the exploitation of various informal institutions and deeply rooted structural differences, such as gender, caste, ethnicity, mobility or geographical origin, has fuelled a "race to the bottom" functional to the reproduction of labour as a flexible, disposable and "cheap" commodity.

Martinez-Novo (2004) stresses the relevance of gender and ethnicity in segmenting labour engaging in export agricultural production in Mexico. Ngai (2005) highlights the relevance of gender and mobility in shaping the identity of Chinese working classes engaging in export manufacturing, and my own work on the Indian export-oriented garment industry has mapped the distinct use of multiple "traditional" structures of power to reproduce and tighten control over the Indian workforce (see Mezzadri, 2008).

This process of *informalization* of labour has generated a vast footloose proletariat who live in a "Global Factory" (Chang, 2009), but whose modes of existence are increasingly complex and varied (Bernstein, 2007). By 2006, according to Mike Davis (quoted in Bernstein, 2007, p. 5), this proletariat was "one billion strong and growing, making it the fastest growing and most unprecedented social class on earth".

After bearing the brunt of the neoliberal capitalist logic for so long, it is somehow paradoxical that labour must now also bear the brunt of the current crisis of this logic. However, that is clearly the case. On the one hand, a point that is widely discussed, in many developed countries the costs of the crisis of the financial elites have been socialized by the state, while working classes were losing their homes in a context of growing unemployment and insecurity. On the other hand, a point that is less widely discussed, the southern footloose proletariat might pay an even higher price because of the crisis of the system that subjugated it so harshly. The crisis, in fact, is slowly revealing all the contradictions and the limitations of overtly "outward-looking" development strategies.

> After bearing the brunt of the neoliberal capitalist logic for so long, it is somehow paradoxical that labour must now also bear the brunt of the current crisis

In some ways, one could argue that the working poor in many developing regions are going through a crisis that is effectively centuries old. It is a perennial crisis of reproduction, strenuously fought through highly diversified livelihood and survival strategies. However, by imposing export orientation as the *deus ex machina* for successful development and by boosting the process of informalization of labour, neoliberalism has effectively created new vulnerabilities and patterns of dependency for the working poor.

The present crisis of this system is now exposing these vulnerabilities in compelling ways. This is the case even in China and India, the two countries which, according to many observers, have benefited the most from export orientation, exploiting their huge reservoirs of cheap labour. In China, it is reported that tens of millions of migrants have started their exodus to return to the rural hinterland, abandoning the buzzing urban industrial areas of the workshop of the world. The *hukou* (household registration) system, establishing a two-tier citizenship system, welcomes the Chinese rural migrant proletariat in the city only when it is employed.

By the same token, the Indian labour employed in export industries in many urban industrial areas seems to be making its way back to the poor states of the Hindi belt such as Bihar and Uttar Pradesh, where its largest share comes from. The exodus of the "disposable workers" has started; it is hard to predict its impact in different developing regions and – within each region – its implications for either the urban or the rural economy.

Focusing specifically on India, the exodus of migrant workers employed by export companies already seems to be accompanied by other trends that negatively affect labour. Workers facing retrenchment but deciding to stay in the city, for instance, will increase the vast pool of slum-dwellers that Indian metropolises adjust to, need, hide and exploit in the urban informal or shadow economy. Decreasing opportunities in the export-based factory realm of production might lead to increasing shares of subcontracting to informal units, further fragmenting domestic supply chains which are already very complex and layered. Rough estimates indicate that by the time the crisis hit, if direct employment in export units could be set at around 6.5 million workers, there were already some 15 million workers indirectly incorporated into export production (Kumar et al., 2009).

According to Jayati Ghosh, the crisis would lead to an increase in the use of home-based workers in various light manufacturing activities, ranging from textile, garments, electronics, gems and jewellery. This is likely to have a very uneven gender impact, as generally Indian home-based labour tends to be primarily female. Prior to the crisis, estimates indicated that over half of the 15 million female informal workers in India were involved in home-based work for different types of industry (see Ghosh's contribution in Kumar et al., 2009). Now, this number may skyrocket even further, signalling a deepening of gender segregation in labour markets.

Therefore, in India, not only is the crisis likely to boost the pace of the process of informalization further, but it also seems to be significantly reshaping and recrafting its patterns. At the moment, evidence suggests a movement away from the factory realm of production, and towards an increasing use of petty commodity production and household labour. Petty commodity production is often used as a cushion against different types of economic shocks. Organized in small clusters in many parts of the subcontinent, the particular resilience of this type of production can be partially attributed to its ability to shape what have been defined by some as social and economic "networks of survival".

Evidence suggests a movement away from the factory realm of production, and towards an increasing use of petty commodity production and household labour

In the context of the present crisis, a partial substitution of casual and precarious factory labour with informal petty production would effectively entail a substitution of wage labour with disguised forms of wage labour, causing a further fragmentation of Indian working classes, a further splintering of the informal proletariat according to multiple lines of socio-economic differentiation, and a further move away from potential attempts to organize this proletariat in meaningful ways. As, once more, the crisis of capital turns into a crisis of labour, and the "race to the bottom" continues, here the bottom seems to be worryingly moving further and further down, crafting new aggressive interplays between informality and poverty.

References

Bernstein, H. 2007. "Capital and labour from centre to margins". Keynote address for conference, *Living on the margins – Vulnerability, exclusion and the state in the informal economy*, Cape Town, 26–28 Mar. 2007. Available at http://www.povertyfrontiers.org/ev_en.php?ID=1953_201&ID2=DO_TOPIC [10 Dec. 2009].

Chang, D. 2009. "Informalising labour in Asia's Global Factory", in *Journal of Contemporary Asia*, Vol. 39, No. 2, pp. 161–179.

Kumar, R. et al. 2009. *Global financial crisis: Impact on India's poor – some initial perspectives* (India, UNDP). Available at http://data.undp.org.in/FinancialCrisis/FinalFCP.pdf [11 Dec. 2009].

Martinez-Novo, C. 2004. "The making of vulnerabilities: Indigenous day labourers in Mexico's neoliberal agriculture", in *Global Studies in Culture and Power*, Vol. 11, pp. 215–239.

Mezzadri, A. 2008. "The rise of neoliberal globalization and the 'new old' social regulation of labour: The case of Delhi garment sector", in *Indian Journal of Labour Economics*, Vol. 51, No. 4, pp. 603–618.

Ngai, P. 2005. *Made in China: Women factory workers in a global workplace* (Durham, Duke University Press).

Alessandra Mezzadri is lecturer in Development Studies at the School of Oriental and African Studies (SOAS), University of London, where she teaches in the MSc Development Studies and in the MSc Globalisation and Development programmes. Her research work focuses on neoliberalism, global industrial restructuring and their impact on labour in developing regions. Her area of expertise is India.

Greece-bashing is hiding the obvious: Monetary union urgently needs economic union

Ronald Janssen

"Bashing the Greeks" has become a very popular sport these days. The main thought on the minds of the financial markets as well as a lot of politicians in Europe is that Greece has only itself to blame for the trouble it is in. After entering monetary union by rigging the statistics, it is argued, Greece went on a huge "spending binge", making public finances unsustainable. This is now even threatening to undermine the financial stability of European monetary union as such. The more "moderate" version of this sort of thinking suggests that Greece should take its medicine and drastically cut all government expenditure and all wages (in both the public and the private sectors). The less "moderate" version simply says that Greece should never have been allowed to join the monetary union in the first place and should now be thrown out of it.

Undoubtedly, Greece does have some "demons" that it needs to tackle, such as the functioning of its statistical office and the transparency of public sector pay. However, the sort of thinking now being developed in Europe is overly simplistic and is a recipe for disaster, not only for Greece but also for workers throughout Europe. Let us examine some of the inconsistencies and contradictions surrounding the case of Greece.

Don't blame the speculators, blame the Greek "fundamentals"

The financial markets' attacks on Greece have not come out of the blue. After all, if Greece is under attack because of its deficit running at 12 per cent of GDP, there are others with a comparably high deficit, such as the United Kingdom or the United States. And even if the Greek deficit has doubled over the past year, almost all other countries in Europe have done the same to prevent a new Great Depression. So why Greece and why right now? The answer is that, since the beginning of November 2009,

> *Even if the Greek deficit has doubled over the past year, almost all other countries in Europe have done the same to prevent a new Great Depression*

central bankers and finance ministers have been spreading negative rumours, with the European Central Bank (ECB) no longer providing liquidity in return for Greek government bonds and the finance ministers of the Euro Group writing a letter which was leaked to the press, urging emergency consolidation measures. This "megaphone diplomacy" focused the financial markets' attention on Greece. In return, central bankers and finance ministers gained a powerful ally (including the same Wall Street agencies that previously gave AAA ratings to "toxic assets") in pushing through their policy agenda: enormous pressure from financial markets to cut deficits, expenditure and wages, not only in Greece but also in other countries.

Governments saving banks, not saving themselves

There is a major double standard at work here. Governments, realizing that banks were caught in a vicious circle of their own making, massively bailed out the banking sector. In Europe alone, the stunning amount of €3 trillion (3,000 billion) in state support was mobilized, and this without much in the way of conditions, such as keeping the credit flow to the economy going. In fact, and thanks to central banks pumping liquidity into the banking sector at zero interest rates, banking profits (and bonuses!) are as high as they were before the crisis! Greece – and others are likely to follow – now finds itself in a similar situation: financial markets, fearing a default, are bidding up interest rates, thereby actually increasing the risk of a default. As was the case for the banks, this vicious circle can only be broken by a powerful and convincing European intervention. Europe, however, seems to prefer to leave Greece out on a limb or, alternatively, is only willing to promise help if Greece (which has a socialist government!) implements a standard liberal programme of cutting wages and reducing the size and the role of the state.

Rewarding the speculators

By showing such reluctance to close ranks with Greece against financial market herd behaviour, Europe is actually rewarding the speculators and boosting their profits. With the price of credit default swaps on Greek sovereign debt soaring, hedge funds are making big bucks on their credit default positions, even or especially if these are "naked" credit default positions (in other words, without hedge funds actually holding Greek sovereign debt). And the same goes for operations on futures markets, where banks and funds are selling Greek sovereign debt, hoping to pick the papers back up again later when prices have collapsed further. Hidden behind the dogmatic "no bail-out" attitude of financial Europe is the very pragmatic policy of continuing to redistribute income and profits to those who caused the crisis in the first place. This, by the way, is not only true in a general sense. Indeed, there are more and more reports that Goldman Sachs – after setting up, for a big fee, a structure that enabled Greece to hide part of its debt – is now heavily involved in betting against Greece.

Greece not doing enough?

Greece has already announced a tough consolidation programme, promising to cut the deficit this year alone by 4 per cent of GDP. Even Germany, a traditional champion of fiscal consolidation, never went that far in so short a period of time. Moreover, Greece is also detailing the measures taken to back up this consolidation effort. These do concern public jobs and wage freezes (for the higher incomes), but also measures to tax the rich (reintroduction of a tax on high fortunes, raising tax revenue on business profits). Nevertheless, this is not enough to appease European politicians and finance ministers. (A related issue is that they may not like a progressive consolidation programme targeting the rich and wealthy.) Instead, Greece in their view needs to gush "blood, sweat and tears". Again, a cynic might observe that if Greece did what it was told and cut everything (much as the US Treasury Secretary Andrew Mellon advised in the Great Depression that all businesses, farmers and workers should be allowed to go bankrupt), it would in any case be plunged into an economic depression. As a consequence, relative debt would still remain high, since what was being gained on the side of the nominator (lower deficit) would be lost on the side of the denominator (falling GDP).

In short, Europe is on a collision course with itself. Europe already seems to have forgotten the important lesson from the financial crisis that casino capitalism urgently needs to be tamed. Instead, some policy circles inside Europe are actually using financial market herd behaviour to push through a neoliberal model that otherwise would be hard to achieve in European democracies. Europe is also completely losing sight of the fact that the internal market is an integrated and mutually dependent economy. The debt of Greece and some other countries, such as Spain, is held to a large extent by British, French and German banks, implying that any default would be costly for these banks. And if orthodox economists succeed in inflicting a long depression on the South of the monetary union, who will be buying the export goods from those countries forming the European core?

Europe is also completely losing sight of the fact that the internal market is an integrated and mutually dependent economy

So instead of this simplistic and populist "Greece-bashing", Europe should urgently develop instruments promoting solidarity between member states against the global casino. We need a common Euro bond limiting speculation on sovereign debt and breaking this cycle of self-fulfilling prophecy organized by the financial markets. We need major European investment programmes, making it possible to offset the contractionary impact of fiscal consolidation plans in Greece and other countries. We need a bigger European budget so that differences in business cycles between member states can be smoothed out without wages having to play the role of the "single variable for adjustment". We need a European ratings agency to break the monopoly of Wall Street agencies which are too often biased in favour of free markets and against labour. We need an ECB that respects the European Treaty and supports member states' finances in the same way as it supports the banking sector. If the ECB continues to relieve the banking sector by buying and holding their "toxic assets", then the ECB should also announce that it will continue to take in BBB-rated sovereign bonds from countries such as Greece. Finally, we need a European Central Bank which raises its inflation target from "less than 2 per cent" to a range of "at least 3 per cent and maximum 4 per cent", thereby increasing the potential impact of wage adaptability on the economy without having to resort to deflationary wage cuts.

Ronald Janssen works as an economic adviser in Brussels.

Riding your luck and adopting the right policies: Why the Australian economy has rebounded strongly

Robert Kyloh

The global economic crisis that commenced in 2008 has had devastating effects across rich and poor nations. But the impact on growth, employment and incomes has not been uniform across countries. Economic performance has depended critically on the policy response adopted by governments. Other authors writing for the Global Labour Column have made a convincing case for an income-led growth strategy in response to the recession. At least one country has clearly demonstrated the benefits of this approach.

Australia is often referred to as the "lucky country". The recent economic performance of this resource-rich nation has helped reinforce this notion. Indeed, recent economic achievements down under may be partly due to the good fortune of rebounding commodity prices and expanding Asian markets, particularly China. These developments encouraged a pick-up in private investment expenditure towards the end of 2009 and are expected to exert a positive influence on economic growth in the period ahead. But they are not the main reasons Australia avoided a recession during the global economic crisis. In fact, the terms of trade actually moved against Australia in the last 18 months and net exports detracted significantly from economic growth in 2009. Rather, the main factors keeping economic growth positive were public policies that boosted the disposable incomes of low- and middle-income families when aggregate demand was plummeting.

The Australian economy has performed better than any other advanced economy since the onset of the global financial crisis. Real GDP increased by 1.4 per cent in 2009 (compared to 2008) and by 2.7 per cent through the year to the December quarter 2009. By comparison it is estimated that advanced economies as a group contracted by 3.2 per cent in 2009, and the global economy contracted for the first time in the post-war period. Moreover, the Australian labour market is rebounding strongly, creating 200,000 additional jobs between August 2009 and February 2010. As of February 2010 the national unemployment rate stood at 5.3 per cent, having declined 0.5

percentage points from the recent high in July 2009. This has led to suggestions that the unemployment rate may have already peaked at the moderate level of 5.8 per cent. This will be a remarkable achievement given earlier expectations. Back in May 2009, when the National Budget for 2009–10 was announced, the Government had projected that unemployment could peak at around 10 per cent without any stimulus measures. Much of the contraction in labour demand in 2008–09 took the form of declines in average hours worked rather than increases in unemployment. But recent trends suggest the jobs market has stabilized and a significant proportion (60 per cent) of the new jobs being created are full time.

The Australian labour market is rebounding strongly, creating 200,000 additional jobs between August 2009 and February 2010

The Australian Government introduced fiscal stimulus measures in three main stages: in October 2008, February 2009 and May 2009. The total package contained a wide variety of measures which can be summarized under three broad headings: first, increased transfer payments to low- and middle-income groups which were rapidly disbursed and had an almost immediate impact on consumption expenditure, retail sales and economic growth; second, relatively rapid investments in social infrastructure, including schools, health and housing; and third, major new investments in economic infrastructure, which are more medium term in nature. The stimulus measures adopted were broadly consistent with proposals made by the Australian Council of Trade Unions.

A striking feature of the Australian response to the crisis, compared to that of most other countries, has been the emphasis placed on increasing the disposable incomes of low- and middle-income groups with a very high marginal propensity to consume. This approach is in complete conformity with the key aspects of the ILO Global Jobs Pact with its emphasis on income-led growth and improvements in the social floor.

The initial substantive fiscal response to the global financial crisis was a 10.4 billion Australian dollar ($A) package of measures announced on the 14 October 2008. This package was tightly targeted at sectors of the economy showing particular weakness in the early stages of the downturn – household consumption and dwelling investment. In the second quarter of 2008 household consumption expenditure had recorded its first decline in 15 years. This package included one-off additional payments to pensioners of $A1,400 for singles and $A2,100 for couples. (Australia has a universal pension scheme with flat-rate benefits funded by general taxation. This is supplemented by private contributory pensions or what is called "superannuation" in Australia.)

The package also included additional payments of A$1,000 to eligible persons providing care to the aged or disabled and for each child in families receiving the Family Tax Benefit (which is a means-tested transfer payment received by low- and middle-income families).

This package of measures generated significant multiplier effects as the payments were timed to be received by credit-constrained families in the lead-up to the year-end holiday period, thus limiting the leakages expected through increased savings. In Australia, like other advanced economies, consumption expenditure comprises around 60 per cent of GDP and has important implications for other areas of expenditure, including private investment. At the time of its announcement, the Government projected that the above strategy would boost real GDP growth by between 0.5 per cent and 1 per cent over a period of several quarters.

In early February 2009, the Government announced a second A$42 billion fiscal stimulus package. This included over A$12 billion to fund a range of additional one-off transfer payments targeted at a variety of low- and middle-income groups. Well over half the population of Australia received payments of just under A$1,000 as part of this initiative. These one-off increases in transfer payments were supplemented by major revisions to the aged pension system and other social security benefits in May 2009. These reforms have resulted in substantial permanent increases in welfare payments. The net impact of these revisions will be to increase expenditure on pensions and related social security payments by A$14.4 billion over the next four years.

The above-mentioned increases in transfer payments, along with reduced interest rates resulting from monetary easing, helped retail sales remain buoyant in Australia in the first half of 2009 when economic and employment growth were at their weakest. The stimulus measures, and in particular the direct payments to low- and middle-income households, have also had a significant impact on business and consumer confidence. Consumer confidence recovered strongly in mid-2009 and has been well above its long-term average level since the latter part of 2009, while business confidence is now at its strongest level in over seven years.

The stimulus measures, and in particular the direct payments to low- and middle-income households, have also had a significant impact on business and consumer confidence

The effects of the first stage of the stimulus packages, involving increased transfers, are now abating. But the second and third phases of the stimulus – involving significant investments in what was colloquially referred to as "shovel ready" social infrastructure projects and longer term national building projects like roads, rail networks and energy conservation – are now under way. One critical aspect of the social infrastructure projects involved a A$14.7 billion investment in school infrastructure and maintenance. This was part of the February 2009 stimulus package and included resources to build or upgrade libraries and halls in every primary school and special school in the country, to significantly expand the number of schools with science laboratories and language learning centres, and to ensure every Australian school has resources to maintain and renew school buildings. Further substantial investments in universities and tertiary education were provided in the May 2009 measures, thus furthering the education revolution in Australia.

Deep economic contractions can permanently reduce an economy's growth prospects through the erosion of skills and capital. The public investments in education plus other social and physical infrastructure were designed to mitigate these effects and to position Australia for economic recovery by raising productivity and expanding the supply-side potential. Fortunately, with the downturn now expected to be more shallow and the labour market recovering rapidly, the long-term output loss should be mild and the economy should return to capacity sooner than expected.

Australia is in the vanguard of the economic recovery among advanced economies because it took swift and concerted action to boost the disposable incomes of working families and welfare recipients, who spent rather than saved these payments and thus sparked recovery. Australia has demonstrated the potential of an income-led growth strategy as advocated by the ILO. It pays to be lucky and also adopt the right strategies.

Robert Kyloh is Senior Economic Adviser in the Integration Department of the ILO. He has previously worked for the Bureau of Workers' Activities in the ILO and the Australian Government.

PART IV

Can the economic crisis lead to a redefinition of labour strategies?

Unions and the crisis: Ways ahead?

Gregory Albo

The political and economic setting facing the union movement today is, perhaps, the most difficult since the Great Depression. Unions had already confronted two decades of unrelenting assault from neoliberal policies of labour market flexibility, austerity and political conservatism. Then, the global financial crisis ripped across the entire world market.

The tally of financial losses is quite staggering. The US Government alone has already committed $9 trillion to its financial sector in various forms to maintain solvency. The sheer magnitude of the debt means that depressed economic conditions are likely to be long-lasting, and the distributional struggles very intense over how the bad debt – "toxic assets" is the euphemism of the day to disguise the massive market failure and incompetency of the financial sector – is destroyed, socialized or inflated away.

The financial chaos is causing untold damage to workers. The ILO has suggested that global job losses could reach as high as $51 million for 2009.

Capitalist strategies

Competitive imperatives will compel capitalist firms (as well as state employers) to restructure workplaces and challenge union contracts. This will build on what is now a three decades-old "employers' offensive".

The offensive emerged in the late 1970s as capitalists attempted to restore company profitability and control over the labour process after considerable erosion over the post-war boom. The rate of profit had fallen by about half over the post-war decades across virtually all zones of the world market. The decline in profit rates coincided with a push by unions and workers to gain an increasing share of output, to expand public services and to address inequalities facing women and racial minorities. These efforts were backed by the largest and longest strike wave in the history of the advanced capitalist countries from the mid-1960s to across the 1970s.

> *Competitive imperatives will compel capitalist firms to restructure workplaces and challenge union contracts*

The capitalist classes responded with a number of strategies to the union militancy and declining profits. At the state level, neoliberal policies from the 1980s on deregulated markets, imposed fiscal austerity, cut welfare, liberalized trade and capital flows and so on. In terms of workplaces, this meant increased "flexibility" in terms of job controls, wages and employment.

Firms have re-organized their labour processes into international production networks and shifted work into low-wage, weak-union production zones. Information and communications technologies have facilitated the introduction of "lean production" intensifying work processes. Employers have broken with "standard" work arrangements and increasingly resort to contingent work arrangements, cheap migrant labour pools and temporary work programmes. In collective bargaining, unions increasingly trade off wage restraint and workplace concessions against job security, agree to co-management schemes for firm competitiveness and even enter into "voluntary recognition agreements" to gain members while giving up the right to strike and other job controls. The employers' offensive has made "competitive unionism" the dominant practice, in both the public and private sectors, in North America.

In terms of wages the focus was on curbing real wage gains for workers and breaking a linkage between productivity gains and annual wage improvements. More of output increases would thus go toward profits.

The economic crisis has made employers even more militant in their demands for wage austerity and concessions. One strategy has been cuts to negotiated health benefits (insurance plans in the United States) for current employees and retirees, as well as other benefits. Another emerging strategy is to redefine – or even walk away from – pension obligations, as has occurred in the steel and auto sectors and in numerous non-unionized companies. Work intensification is also occurring as workers are being pushed to give up time-off, holidays, work breaks and so forth.

New political openings?

Marx argued in *Capital* that each phase of accumulation contained the seeds of its own destruction. The internal contradictions of neoliberalism are now readily apparent: fictitious capital and debt massively growing relative to the growth of productive capacity and the deterioration of public services; wage compression leading to increasingly indebted working classes and unstable conditions for effective demand; the undermining of extra-market regulatory capacities to constrain capitalist competition, speculative bubbles and fraud as an endemic feature of financialization; and huge international payments imbalances reinforcing dependence on the world market while spreading its potential instabilities.

Neoliberal and free market ideology is now totally discredited. But capitalist strategies and government policies are attempting to reconstruct neoliberalism as the basis for again restoring capitalist profitability. This is the political challenge the union movement now faces.

Existing union strategies are neither confrontational enough to challenge capitalist workplace strategies after years of concessions. Nor are they politically ambitious enough to form the necessary anti-capitalist strategies to form the political agendas and organizational capacities to forge an alternative approach to the crisis.

There are, however, several hopeful signs of union renewal that could begin to chart a new direction. In North America, some of this has come from "living wage" struggles led by local labour councils in major cities, in alliance with community groups, to reach out to the low-waged and unorganized, who are predominantly women and people of colour. The mass immigrants' rights May Day protests, as well as the day-to-day campaigns for the protection of non-status workers, have taken place outside the main union movements, but have also led to new linkages and alliances. A number of campaigns – notably some of the anti-privatization struggles around health care, universities and municipal services – have seen successes across several countries. These community–union alliances, often coupled with major campaigns and demonstrations, suggest enormous potential.

A number of campaigns have seen successes across several countries

There also have been interesting examples of a new organizational internationalism amongst unions. The efforts to coordinate aspects of collective bargaining in the steel, auto and health-care sectors, extending from North America to both Europe and Latin America, to confront work issues spread across international production networks, are one example. The campaign against the militantly anti-union Wal-Mart is also suggestive.

In the context of the economic crisis, it is necessary to form a set of demands that might converge across different struggles and sectors to embed an anti-market logic in bargaining that might offset the worst features of the slowdown. In terms of workplace struggles, a core set of campaigns might be: (1) the fight against concessions in wages and benefits; (2) the preservation of negotiated pensions; (3) building in annual reductions in work-time within wage negotiations; (4) support for plant occupations and community seizure of assets, particularly in cases of bankruptcy and firms receiving state subsidies;

and (5) the extension of all other forms of hours reduction in terms of parental leaves, annual holidays, overtime and so forth. A set of union demands directed at the economic crisis is also important: (1) the overhaul or unemployment insurance systems in terms of benefits, principles of eligibility and administration; (2) industrial strategies directed at ecologically responsible production; (3) massive extension of "green jobs" in the culture, leisure and sporting sectors; (4) nationalization of the banking sector; (5) building a national childcare system; (6) nationalization of the transportation sector and development of a national mass transit strategy; and (7) the establishment of a national housing programme.

Ways ahead

These types of demands, of course, have been percolating through the union and socialist movement for some time. They will depend on reversing the decline of the union movement and the wider impasse of the Left. Working-class political organization has in the past achieved a great deal: leading decolonization struggles; campaigning for the expansion of freedoms and equality to women and racial and sexual minorities; improving wages and benefits; and agitating for the extension of universal welfare states.

The social forces that achieved these gains are now quite something else: the communist parties have all but disappeared even in places where they once held power (or they have made their peace with capitalism as in China); the social democratic parties now chart a "Third Way" and no longer even pose a reform agenda to neo/liberalism; unions are in retreat; and many civil society movements have evolved into professionalized NGOs navigating the grant economy. The central political coordinates for labour movements over the last century – being for or against the Russian revolution, attempting a vanguard seizure of the existing state apparatus or reforming it piecemeal, and conceiving unions as primarily the industrial wing of this or that political party – no longer provide any kind of map for the struggles unions and workers now confront.

For a brief moment, it seemed as if a decentralized "network politics" – a "movement of movements" – would provide, if not a map for the future, a renewed political capacity for the Left. It was represented in the hopeful "Teamsters and Turtles" slogan of the heady days of the anti-globalization movement. But apart from episodic demonstrations and annual social justice fairs, the networks have broken apart more often than they have provided new organizational nodes. There has been almost a complete lack of organizational grounding in the day-to-day struggles of working-class communities, workplaces and unions.

This "anti-power" politics is now being eclipsed by new political experiments beginning from – and not against – organizational commitments to unions and political parties. In Latin America, this has taken place under the banner of building twenty-first century socialism in a number of countries. A "new" New Left appears to be emerging from the margins in France, Greece, Germany, Portugal and other places as well.

From their anchor in workplace struggles and in particular communities, a renewed union movement is a crucial component of such a new Left. Indeed, in representing the deep diversity of workers and their issues – in terms of gender, racial background, sexual diversity and so forth – unions have been leading society in this area over the period of neoliberalism rather than following it. Moving on will require forming new political capacities and an organizational openness and creativity that the Left in North America has not shown for some time. That realization is always the point of a new beginning.

Gregory Albo is Associate Professor, Department of Political Science, York University, Toronto. He teaches courses on the foundations of political economy, Canadian political economy, democratic administration and alternatives to capitalism.

New challenges for labour as growth prospects fade away

Cédric Durand

With the current crisis, economies and societies are entering a period of institutional shake up which occurs in initial conditions that are *much* more disadvantageous to labour than during the crisis of the 1970s. At the same time, a paradigm shift is emerging as growth prospects are fading away in advanced economies. The onset of this dispensation poses serious challenges to the labour movement and progressive political economists; this article attempts to address them and to stimulate debate.

The great contemporary crisis takes place in an environment which is radically different from the great profitability crisis of the 1970s. On the one hand, the post-world war period had allowed labour to build a strong bargaining power position. On the contrary, since the 1980s, neoliberal policies have successfully weakened its position. The combined disciplinary effects of a growing reserve army of labour, new managerial principles of controlled autonomy reinforced by information technology, increasingly heterogeneous employment norms, spatial splintering of production and an increased exposure to multidimensional competitive pressures have sapped labour combativeness. Rising inequalities in favour of a thin layer of super rich and the dramatic decrease in the number of strikes are symptomatic of the retreat of labour in rich countries.

Rising inequalities in favour of a thin layer of super rich and the dramatic decrease in the number of strikes are symptomatic of the retreat of labour in rich countries

On the other hand, the post-war boom appears in retrospect to have been a golden age for capitalist accumulation when, contrastingly, the past 30 years represent an age of decline. The average annual growth in high-income economies has fallen from 5.5 per cent in the 1960s to a mere 1.64 per cent during the first decade of the new century (see figure below), while the investment rate is also slowing, from 25.1 per cent in the 1970s down to 20.5 per cent in the 2000s.

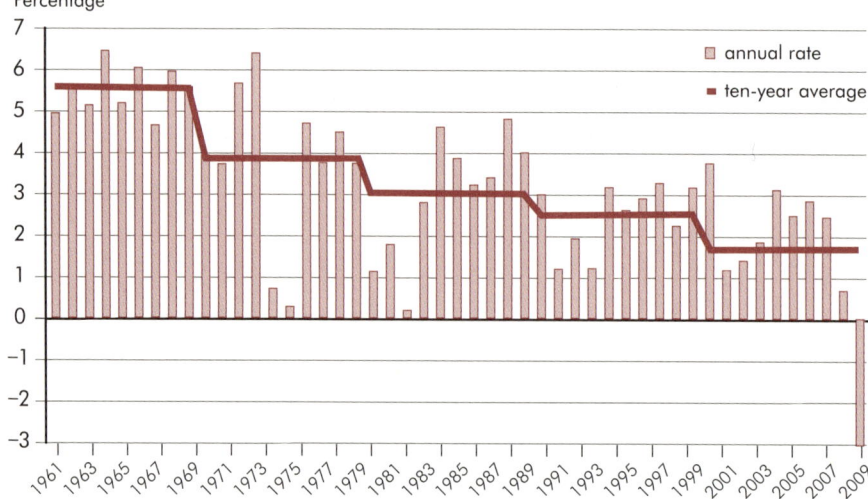

Annual GDP growth in high-income economies

Sources: For 1960–2008, "High-income OECD" World Development Indicators, World Bank, 2009, http://data.worldbank.org/indicator; for 2009, "Advanced Economies", World Economic Outlook Database, IMF, April 2010, http://www.imf.org/external/pubs/ft/weo/2010/01/weodata/index.aspx

The parallel trends of labour retreat and capital decline in advanced economies suggest that what is at stake beyond the crisis is not only the conditions of the recovery, but the shaping of a new socio-economic path where the promises of unlimited progress in well-being through growing mass consumption would not be pertinent any more. Of course, the dynamics at play in developing countries are different; processes associated with "catching up" still allow some important margin for growth. However, focusing on the advanced economies is important to capturing this paradigm shift, which takes place at two different levels.

At a first level, we observe that the world economy is locked in a neoliberal institutional configuration that hinders accumulation. The rise of new industrial countries and liberalization of trade led to structural excess capacity and cut-throat global competition in core industries, as is exemplified by the emblematic case of the automotive industry. In addition, the short-term financial returns required by market investors deprive firms of the financial resources required to invest. Finally, depleted labour income and recurrent financial crises tend to depress demand and increase uncertainty, both of which also weaken the incentives to invest. In short, the competition regime, corporate governance structures and demand dynamics together produce a sluggish accumulation regime. Theoretically, significant changes in economic policies allowing a more coordinated and stronger growth path are perfectly feasible. Politically, things are far more complicated: such changes would require a significant shift in the balance of power to the detriment of financial interests and a coordination of government policies at the regional and global levels in order to adjust accumulation paths and limit structural excess capacity.

However, at a second level, it is necesary to stress that even a significant restructuring of global governance will probably not be sufficient to initiate a new economic boom in advanced countries. First, an ageing population, rising environmental costs and the increasing scarcity of key natural resources are triggering an appreciation of input prices that will constrain growth through reduced profits and/or wages. Second, these economies have not been able to find a successor to the techno-economic paradigm of the "golden age" that would be compatible with the pursuit of a rapid expansion of capitalism. On the one hand, the promised wave of expansion associated with innovations in IT collapsed in 2001 and has not since found a way to take off again. This stalling has to do with the specific characteristics of knowledge: there is a deep contradiction between, on the one side, the defence of intellectual property rights in the name of profit, which hinders the diffusion of knowledge, and, on the other, the fact that societies need and want to take advantage of the highly beneficial dynamics of knowledge diffusion, whose cost is close to zero. On the other hand, the demand associated with social needs is more and more oriented towards services such as health care, education and leisure, where the prospects for productivity gains are scarce, unlike in manufacturing.

Growth prospects in advanced industrial countries are seriously fading because of the contradictions of neoliberalism on the one hand and rising input costs, the inconsistency of the IT techno-paradigm and the evolution of social needs (and associated demand) on the other. Such a diagnosis has tremendous implications for labour, in particular the likely intensification of its antagonism with capital.

Growth prospects in advanced industrial countries are seriously fading

During the post-war era, many factors contributed to the diffusion of social benefits, from regular wage increases to the reduction of inequalities typical of Fordism. But rapid growth was the necessary condition for – as well as a result of – this configuration, which was relatively favourable to workers. On the contrary, in an era characterized by low growth and by dull prospects as far as the employment rate is concerned, the distributional conflict between wages and profits is intensifying, while the bargaining power of labour has deteriorated. Moreover, in order to escape exhaustion tendencies, over-accumulated capital is exploring further forms of "accumulation by dispossession", cutting or limiting the public's access to resources, spaces and public services, while socializing losses through recurrent bail-outs.

The labour movement needs to reposition itself in order to face these serious challenges. Assessing the possible trajectories out of growth is a new frontier for political economy, appealing for a progressive revival of the issue of the stationary state – i.e. the end of capital accumulation – discussed by the classical economists. In this context, union claims also need to evolve. A massive rollback of inequalities and a broadened access to common goods have to be achieved in order to render fair and acceptable a renouncement to the permanent objective of rising wages combined with a large-scale transformation of employment (e.g. destruction of non-sustainable jobs, new jobs in care sectors, reduction of working-time). Finally, unions, social movements, political parties and non-governmental organizations need to enter a phase of substantive re-articulation. Because of the dramatic retreat of shop-floor labour bargaining power, the centrality of class conflict "à la Marx", namely located in the production site, is likely to be further challenged and will not be sufficient to obtain a post-growth economic settlement favourable to labour. But a greater importance of class conflicts "à la Polanyi", i.e. broader forms of resistance against the macro and social forms of capitalist domination, may help to achieve such a desirable outcome. At the local as well as at the global level, unions need then to engage more systematically in broader alliances with social and political actors to promote effectively labour interests throughout the emergent post-growth paradigm.

Cédric Durand is an associate professor at Paris 13 University and a member of the Centre d'Économie Paris-Nord (CEPN) and of the Centre d'Études des Modes d'Industrialisation (CEMI-EHESS). He participates in the editorial board of the critical review Contretemps (http://www.contretemps.eu). Cédric wrote his Ph.D. on the trajectory of the metallurgical sector during post-Soviet transformation in the Russian Federation; he has published several articles on post-Soviet capitalism and on the internationalization of the retail industry.

Making its voice heard: A role for the labour movement in policies for recovery

Andrew Watt

Let us be optimistic and assume for the sake of argument that the economic crisis is behind us and the world's economies will return slowly to "trend" growth. What are the main challenges facing policy-makers and, especially, the labour movement? There is the urgent issue of rethinking our financial system, which is key to averting a relapse into crisis down the line, and the need in the medium run to manage the transition to an ecologically sustainable growth model. Between these two priorities are a set of intertwined challenges on which I would like to focus here: getting unemployment down, lowering fiscal deficits and reducing inequalities. All these are vital if we are to move towards a sustainable economic and social growth model that serves the interests of the many, not the few.

The good news is that these aims are not mutually exclusive. On the contrary, there is a set of policies – a policy mix – that can achieve them all simultaneously. The bad news is that, in many cases, such policies do not seem to be high priorities on policy-makers' to-do lists. Getting the balance between monetary, fiscal and wage policies right over time and across countries is not quite everything, but it is central to addressing the grave challenges that face us and avoiding a backlash in favour of reactionary policies.

What would that policy mix look like?

Key to getting both unemployment and fiscal deficits down is returning to faster economic growth. Merely getting back to "trend" growth rates – in developed countries 2–3 per cent a year – will not be enough. For the foreseeable future, this requires the maintenance of aggressive stimulus measures in most countries (I shall return to the "most" caveat).

Key to getting both unemployment and fiscal deficits down is returning to faster economic growth

It is vital that the world's leading central banks uniformly commit to keeping interest rates at or near zero for the foreseeable future and that fiscal expansion is initially maintained as far as possible.

But what about the risk of inflation and the problems of overburdened government budgets? In fact, both factors are arguments in favour of sustained expansionary monetary policy. Government budgets are indeed in a parlous state in most countries, virtually "inviting" welfare state cutbacks. Low interest rates are absolutely vital to bringing them back close to balance. Lower policy rates help to keep the interest paid by governments down, thus limiting debt-servicing costs. They stimulate real economic growth and, not least, bring about a desirable rise in the rate of price increases. Why desirable? Because inflation is substantially below target, and faster inflation raises the nominal rate of economic growth, which is decisive for fiscal consolidation. Specifically in the euro area, a faster average rate of inflation would also dramatically ease adjustment problems for those countries (like Greece and Spain) that have to reduce their relative wages and prices. And if you are worried about bubbles, regulate the markets – don't kill the economy with high interest rates.

Given an extended period of low interest rates, what must fiscal policy-makers do?

Deficits will be reduced only when the economy picks up sufficiently for unemployment to fall. In the short run this means that most countries still need expansionary fiscal policies. With monetary policy still up against a zero bound and with the banking system still sluggish, fiscal policy has a vital role to play in sustaining demand and in channelling spending towards socially desirable outcomes, such as lower inequality or the transition to a low-carbon economy. At the same time, credible consolidation plans should be announced now and foreseen with an appropriate "trigger". It makes no sense to use an arbitrary date, such as "the start of 2011", as a starting point. Instead a sensible real-economic trigger, a certain output or employment target, tailored to national conditions, should be used.

A key challenge for the labour movement is to ensure that, in qualitative terms, these consolidation measures are favourable to working people. This implies a focus on strengthening revenue capacity, and deflecting the tax burden away from labour and on to capital, high incomes and material resources. Specifically, progressive political forces should unite behind calls for a financial transactions tax (at international or European level) and for the introduction of an EU carbon tax with a levy at the external border.

Should all countries run the same expansionary fiscal policies?

No. Those countries with relatively low deficits/debts and with current account surpluses should do more for longer to stimulate their economies. In the euro area this means Germany, but also Austria and the Netherlands. Faster demand growth in these countries would be good for employment there and would dramatically ease the adjustment issues facing the euro area. Similar considerations apply at the global level to China and Japan; in the case of the former, this could best be achieved via a return to a policy of steady exchange-rate appreciation. Fiscally constrained countries must attempt as far as possible to sustain demand while coping with their adjustment problems; clamping down on tax avoidance would raise revenue without depressing demand so much. Demand and price deflation is almost always the most costly strategy. There is a better way.

And what about wage policy, unions' "core business"?

It is both simple and hard at the same time. In a state of equilibrium, real wages should rise at the same rate as labour productivity, i.e. nominal wages at that rate plus an allowance for "desirable" inflation. In most advanced capitalist countries, real wages did not keep pace with labour productivity during much of the neoliberal period; rising profits, siphoned off by the financial sector and by CEOs and channelled into speculation, were a major cause of the crisis. In a nutshell, this happened because the institutional structures that underpinned the balanced growth, and especially the productivity–wage nexus, of the Fordist era were destroyed by neoliberalism. Modern equivalents need to be found. No general blueprint for this can be given, but progressive governments and union movements have to start designing and developing such mechanisms. Some useful points of departure include establishing or strengthening minimum wages and governmental support for collective bargaining institutions (e.g. extending the coverage of representative collective agreements or reducing free-riding by charging non-member firms and workers a bargaining levy). An important role can be played by measures to reduce price pass-through by companies: there is a strong progressive case to be made for a smart deregulation of product and services markets to reduce firms' pricing power and thus raise real wages.

It is very important to find the right path for nominal wages. In the short run, the concern is to avoid deflationary wage developments (concession bargaining) which will hamper, not aid, recovery, as generalized price deflation may take hold. In the medium run, as the recovery hopefully strengthens, nominal wage increases in line with the above rule will help underpin continued expansionary monetary policies.

Within a monetary union, the issues are rather different. As recent events have shown, persistent divergences from the nominal wage norm (in both directions) can build up in the member countries over a longer period. Then suddenly they require correction – one-sidedly by deficit countries – in the worst possible context, a deep economic and fiscal crisis, to which the imbalances were an important contributing factor. The key step here is for the surplus countries to engineer faster wage growth. Once again, the policy goals are not in conflict; a good way to achieve this in the short term is to run a more expansionary fiscal policy. At the same time, deficit countries need to reduce their relative price levels. There is a better way than fiscal contraction and a deep recession to induce deflation, such as some form of social pact to freeze wages and prices, ideally against a background of faster area-wide inflation.

What can labour hope for?

There is a path out of the crisis, one leading to stable and balanced economic growth and a steady return to lower unemployment, sound public finances and rising real wage incomes. There are no insuperable goal conflicts or fundamental problems in moving on to this trajectory, and labour's key interest must be to get onto it. However, for this to occur, the key areas of monetary, fiscal and wage policy need to be well coordinated with one another, both across time and space. The coordination mechanisms that do exist at the supranational (European, global) level are weak (the EU Macroeconomic Dialogue), flawed (the Stability and Growth Pact) and/or nascent (the G20). Meanwhile the forces of globalization undermine those coordination mechanisms that were, or still are, effective at the national level. Charting out the required policy mix is relatively easy, and positive steps are possible even with the limited coordination structures currently in place. What will be harder is moving towards newer, more effective, coordination structures that permit economically efficient, socially just and ecologically sustainable outcomes over an extended time horizon.

> **Neoliberalism has been decisively weakened by the crisis, but its proponents are regrouping**

Neoliberalism has been decisively weakened by the crisis, but its proponents are regrouping. There is still an opportunity for labour to make its voice heard in a progressive restructuring of global, European and national structures. It has a vital interest in doing so. It has good arguments. It must also shout, and the others must be persuaded – or forced – to listen.

Andrew Watt is Senior Researcher at the European Trade Union Institute (ETUI). He edits the ETUI Policy Brief on European Economic and Employment Policy and is co-editor of a recent book, After the crisis: Towards a sustainable growth model *(ETUI, 2010). He writes a monthly column for the Social Europe Journal.*

Financial crises, the informal economy and workers' unions

Renana Jhabvala

Workers all over the world have been hit by the financial crisis, and unemployment rates, particularly in developed countries, have risen to high levels. Little is known, however, about the effects on the informal workers in developing countries who have no security net or unemployment insurance, and no personal savings cushion to tide them over the crisis. Even worse, as the crisis deepened and the world began looking for solutions, these workers' voices and concerns were not heard, as their "unemployment rates" were rarely measured. Unemployment in the informal economy cannot be measured by "jobs lost", but rather by income decline, decrease of days of work available and disappearing livelihoods.

The importance of understanding the impact of the global recession on the informal economy cannot be underestimated. The informal economy includes all economic units that are not regulated by the state and all economically active persons who do not receive social protection through their work. The size and significance of the informal economy is tremendous and, in developing regions, the informal economy makes up anywhere from 60 to 90 per cent of the total workforce. Moreover, the formal and informal economies are not entirely distinct. In global value chains, production, distribution and employment can fall at different points on a continuum between pure "formal" relations (i.e. regulated and protected) at one pole and pure "informal" relations (i.e. unregulated and unprotected) at the other, with many intermediate categories in between. Workers and units can also move across the formal–informal continuum and/or operate simultaneously at different points along it. These dynamic linkages of the formal and informal economies highlight the importance of understanding the "informality" of the global economy and recession.

The size and significance of the informal economy is tremendous and, in developing regions, the informal economy makes up anywhere from 60 to 90 per cent of the total workforce

Before the financial crisis the GDP growth rates in the Asian economies were among the highest in the world, with the 2008 growth rate in India being over 9 per cent. Banks in India had been well regulated and so did not undergo the same crises as the Western banks, but because of economic uncertainty they were wary of lending and the credit slowdown added further to the reduction in investment. However, the financial system has become internationally connected and, in January 2008, the Bombay Stock Exchange Index, which had grown 21,000 points, began to fall rapidly. It had fallen to 15,000 points in June 2008 and to 10,500 points in October 2008. This caused a severe shortage of liquidity and a major reduction of investment as the capital of traders and industrialists eroded. At the same time, industries dependent on export began a slow decrease with spiral effects into the rest of the economy. The worst-hit industries were diamonds and other gems and jewels as well as textiles, garments and metalware.

Studies undertaken by the Self-Employed Women's Association (SEWA) in early 2009 and later by Women in Informal Employment: Globalizing and Organizing (WIEGO) found crises in sectors where informality was concentrated. It is estimated that 1–2 per cent of the urban population of the world lives off collecting and recycling paper, cardboard, plastic, glass and metal waste. The earnings of these poorest workers declined considerably worldwide – by more than 50 per cent according to the SEWA survey – as the drop in demand for manufactured goods from developed countries led to a decline in such exports from developing countries which, in turn, led to a decline in demand for recycled waste materials and a drop in the selling price of waste. The net result was that tons of waste materials accumulated on streets or in warehouses, with container loads of waste being stockpiled at harbours or directly going to landfills and incinerators without being sorted for what can be recycled.

SEWA's waste collector members in Ahmedabad said they compensate for lower prices by spending more hours collecting the waste. They used to go in the morning at 5 a.m. but now they start their work at 3 a.m. with the mentality that "someone else will come early and pick it up, so instead I will take it first". Before, the woman of the family would go to pick up the waste, but now they prefer to take more members, especially children of the family, so that more waste is collected. As they are now unable to pay the fees and other expenses for education they have taken them out of school and started to involve the children in waste collection as well as sending them for other income-earning activities.

> *Before, the woman of the family would go to pick up the waste, but now they prefer to take more members, especially children of the family, so that more waste is collected*

Construction was another industry hit worldwide and the main sufferers were the construction workers, who were paid by the day and whose days of work as well as earnings shrank considerably.

Moreover, the Indian survey showed that, whereas normally 85 per cent of women have full-time work of more than 20 days a month, after the crisis only 11 per cent had full-time work. Most of them worked less than 15 days a month and 10 per cent had no work at all. There was also a 30 per cent decline in their daily wages.

One of the first ill-effects of the crisis seemed to be psychological, with increasing conflicts and growing drunkenness, especially among men. Families responded also by reducing their food intake – two meals instead of three, and reducing "expensive" foods like milk or eggs. Some families are going into debt to pay for illnesses or other major expenses; others pulled their children out of school or moved them to cheaper education.

In India, we seem to be coming out of the crisis as the stock market has risen 70 per cent from its low of last year. Industrial production is up, as is employment in many industries such as construction, with the daily wage increasing almost to pre-crisis levels. Although some export-linked industries such as diamonds are still in difficulty, it seems that on the whole Indian informal workers are recovering their employment. However, this does not mean all is well. As the economy recovers, inflation rises too and the prices of staple foods have gone up by 17 per cent in 2009.

From the point of view of the workers, their work lives are full of insecurity. During the crisis, they lost their earnings and had no social safety net to fall back on. As the economy pulls out of the crisis, they face price increases, and without a social protection cover they have to pay for health care and insure themselves against personal crises out of their own earnings and savings.

The world has focused intensively on the financial crisis brought about by the unregulated greed in the financial systems, and will perhaps bring reform within those systems. But for the informal workers, the financial crisis was just one more hurdle in a work-life of continuous insecurity. The solutions lie in more complete systems of social security and a voice for informal workers, who constitute the majority of the workforce today.

Given that informal workers constitute such a large section of the workforce, and that most countries are democratic, with governments being elected on the will of the majority, the real question is, why is a system of social protection not already in place? Such a system would act as a cushion during crises and help workers protect themselves against the volatilities present in the system. The answer to this lies in the balance of power. Today, much of the policies and regulations favour those with capital and especially the larger corporate structures. Those groups which are able to organize and make their voice heard are able to access the countervailing power either through the political system or directly in the market. Unfortunately, informal workers are barely organized today and as a result have neither voice nor representation nor any countervailing power. In fact, they, the most vulnerable of people, become a cushion for the economic system. They are the ones who absorb the most shocks in times of crisis.

The voice of the informal workers needs to be heard, and its effect felt in the political system, in order to start the process of a social safety net for informal workers, which can only happen by organizing. On the ground many trade unions, especially in developing countries, have organized informal workers and brought their voice to the bargaining table. These include agricultural workers and transport workers through the Ghana Trades Union Congress and street vendors in CROC Mexico. SEWA is an example of a national trade union which has reached a membership of 1.2 million informal workers. At the international level networks of organizations of informal workers such as the alliance of Street Vendors (StreetNet), the alliance of home workers (HomeNet) and the newly developing alliances of domestic workers through the IUF and waste collectors alliances are identifying their issues and bringing the voice of informal workers to the international arena. Equally important is the role of WIEGO, which highlights these issues and takes them into the policy arena. However, the scale at which the voice of the informal workers is heard is still far too modest. A fairer international economic system requires a representation in policy-making of the informal workers. This will only happen if workers organize on a large scale.

Renana Jhabvala is one of the early founders of the Self-Employed Women's Association (SEWA). She has been Secretary of SEWA and Chair of SEWA Bank. Presently, she is Chair of SEWA Bharat, which is the all-India federation of SEWA. She has written extensively on the informal economy.

The crisis of social democratic trade unionism in Western Europe

Martin Upchurch

The end of the Second World War in Western Europe ensured political settlements generally inclusive of trade unions. The United Kingdom saw a consolidation of the relationship between the Labour Party and trade unions, while in Germany the SPD entrenched its position as the social democratic "party of labour". The political events that shaped the settlements varied. In France and Italy, the Communist Party had gained credibility in the resistance to German occupation and many workers looked to the Communist Party rather than the reformist Socialist Party. The relationship between a social democratic party and unions was strongest in Sweden, with the Swedish Social Democratic Party (SAP) and the LO (Swedish Trade Union Confederation) forming a stronghold on the political trajectory of that country for many years. Exceptions were Portugal and Spain, where fascist dictatorships lingered on until the 1970s.

The relationship between social democratic parties and the unions was one of mutual interest between the trade union leaders and the party. It was glued together by a compact that assumed that the "party of labour" would grant concessions on the "social wage" in return for the trade union leaders' willingness to hold rank-and-file members in check, especially in inflationary times when wage rises could be restricted. For 30 years at least, the settlement held together in various forms of neo-corporatism, whereby governments (even conservative ones) saw trade unions as legitimate agents, and would "do business" with them. The state supported the institutions of collective bargaining, and the trade union leadership was bureaucratically consumed within the "statization of society" (Panitch, 1986, p. 189).

However, we can define neoliberalism as a specific response by capital to recurrent crises of profitability. This involved a reshaping of the relationship between state, capital and labour whereby Keynesian expansionism could not be sustained in an increasingly integrated world economy. Neoliberalism suggests that trade union wage bargaining adversely affects the

Neoliberalism suggests that trade union wage bargaining adversely affects the "free" market because trade unions raise the price of labour

"free" market because trade unions raise the price of labour. In such circumstances, the social democratic settlements, based as they were on Keynesian commitment to welfare and full employment, were no longer sustainable in a neoliberal vision.

From the 1980s on, the settlements appeared to fragment as social democratic parties and governments sought accommodations with neoliberal orthodoxy through flexible working and decentralization of pay bargaining. Early indications of this tension were already apparent in the "divorce" of the LO union federation from the SAP in 1987.

The joint publication of *The Third Way/Die Neue Mitte* in 1998 by Britain's Tony Blair and Germany's Gerhard Schroeder had signalled a shift in policy direction towards supply-side economic management and worker flexibility. The "old" social democracy was abandoned, to be replaced in Britain by continuing privatization and a distancing between the Labour Party and the unions; in Sweden by the "divorce"; and in Germany by the introduction by the SPD–Green Coalition Government of the Hartz reforms designed to relax the laws of dismissal, and cut back state support for the unemployed and pensioners.

If social democracy was in crisis, so too was the "social democratic" model of trade unionism. The background to the change was a decline in trade union membership, as the effects of neoliberalism began to bite into workers' confidence. Trade union leaderships found it increasingly difficult to gain welfare concessions from governments in return for wage discipline. Where such "pacts" to restrict wage rises have been enabled, they have been justified by the trade union leaders as a policy of the "dented shield" designed to mitigate the worst effects of neoliberal restructuring. They have rarely been accompanied with increases to the "social wage". Such an approach has increased the tensions between social democratic parties in government, the trade union leaders and their rank-and-file members to such an extent that fractures and fissures have begun to appear.

In our book *The crisis of social democratic trade unionism in Western Europe* (by myself, Graham Taylor and Andrew Mathers), we trace the origins of these fractures and examine newly emerging alternative futures for the political representation of trade unions. We do not argue that social democratic trade unionism is at an end, but rather that alternative models of reshaping have emerged. Social democracy itself has morphed into different wings, one represented by Third Way politics which accommodates to neoliberalism and seeks to construct an ideology of partnership between employers and employees in an effort to maintain national business competitiveness (Giddens, 1998). A second wing wishes to return to the values of traditional social democracy and argues that it is possible to reconstruct Keynesian policies. Such a path denies that neoliberal free market ideology is an inevitable product of capitalism's ongoing crisis of profitability. Trade unions adopting this position seek to change the policy of social democratic parties from within. A third approach is cosmopolitan social democracy whereby many trade unions have also responded to globalization by a form of "managed internationalism" arguing for "decent work" through agencies such as the ILO and even the arch-agents of neoliberal policy such as the World Trade Organization, the World Bank and the IMF.

> Many trade unions have also responded to globalization by a form of "managed internationalism" arguing for "decent work"

Our alternative model of radical political unionism, however, identifies a break with social democratic trade unionism and a focus on active agendas which seek to oppose neoliberalism, engage members in social movement activity at grass-roots level, and encourage the use of more innovative and less bureaucratically controlled trade union action. This model is also associated with alignment of unions with new political parties and movements to the left of the social democratic parties. The model reinforces class solidarity at the expense of "national business interest".

The degree of fracture in each country varies. In the United Kingdom, there has long been "formal affiliation" between the Labour Party and the unions, with unions donating yearly up to 60 per cent of the party's funds. However, the Labour Party leadership has sought to downgrade formal power of the unions within the party, and has sought funding from business sources. Unions have moved from power-brokers to internal lobbyists. In the public sector tensions between party and unions have been most acute.

In Germany, the political relationship between the SPD and the unions has been informal but the new fracture is dramatic and focuses on the emergence of Die Linke as a serious party to the left of the SPD. Die Linke was formed from the mass opposition movement to the Hartz reforms of the public sector beginning in 2003. In the 2009 election it gained 76 Bundestag representatives with nearly 12 per cent of the vote. Exit polls suggested that 780,000 former SPD voters switched votes to the new party. Die Linke is a coalition of disaffected SPD members, ex-PDS (the party reformed from the old ruling Communist Party) members in eastern Germany, and far-left activists in the unions.

In France, the traditional fragmentation of political representation of the unions appears to have carried over to new formulations of political and social identity. Opposition to neoliberalism has been highly visible "on the streets", as public sector workers have taken consistent strike action. Of the three main federations, the Confédération française du travail (CFDT) has been most visible in supporting a Third Way position, Force Ouvrière has continued to support Keynesian solutions in defence of the public sector, while the Confédération générale du travail (CGT) has vacillated between support and opposition to neoliberal measures. An interesting feature of contemporary French trade unionism has been the emergence of dissident breakaway unions attached to the Group of 10, such as SUD (Solidaires, Unitaires, Démocratiques). SUD is particularly active in the railways and public sector and, although small, has adopted an anti-neoliberal position and has related to social movements such as the *sans papiers* and the Confédération Paysanne.

In Sweden, the bonds between the union federation and the SAP remain stronger. We can observe a continuing thread of a unique "folk tradition" that has survived outside of other experiences. The peculiarities and specificities of Swedish social movement unionism can thus be seen as a product of a continuing hegemony of social democratic values.

In summary, the crisis of social democracy has transformed into a potential crisis of the social democratic model of trade unionism. This marks a qualitative change from previous crises in which challenges to social democratic trade unionism were always contained within the party or neutralized by the institutions of industrial relations. This is not to argue that these processes of containment and institutionalization no longer exist or no longer work, but rather to suggest that the limits of the process have been breached to various degrees of significance. We detect new formulations of union identity, engagement beyond the workplace, and newly politicized union strategy. Of course, such new formulations remain fragile and open to division, political tension and subsequent reformulation. Nevertheless, we suggest that the continuing adaptation to neoliberalism as a means of capital accumulation by social democratic parties in power will mean a continuation of the crisis, and a parallel "opening up" of workers' organized political dissent within wider civil society.

References

Giddens, A. 1998. *The Third Way: The renewal of social democracy* (Cambridge, Polity).

Panitch, L. 1986. *Working class politics in crisis: Essays on labour and the state* (London, Verso).

Upchurch, M.; Taylor, G.; Mathers, A. 2009. *The crisis of social democratic trade unionism in Western Europe: The search for alternatives* (Aldershot, Ashgate).

Martin Upchurch is Professor of International Employment Relations at Middlesex University Business School, London. He is co-author of The realities of partnership at work *(Palgrave, 2008) and* The crisis of social democratic trade unionism in Western Europe: The search for alternatives *(Ashgate, 2009).*